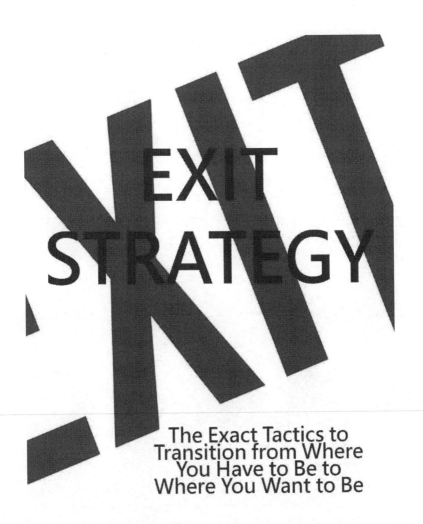

EXIT STRATEGY

The Exact Tactics to
Transition from Where
You Have to Be to
Where You Want to Be

ELLORY WELLS

Mention of specific companies, organizations, people, or authorities in this book does not imply endorsement by the author or the publisher, nor does mention of specific companies, organizations, people, or authorities imply that they endorse this book, its author, or the publisher.

Internet addresses and telephone numbers given in this book were accurate at the time it went to press.

© 2016 by Ellory Wells

If you would like to invite the author to speak at an event for your organization, please contact him via the website below.

www.ellorywells.com

Disclosure of Material Connection: Some of the links in this book are "affiliate links." This means if you click on the link and purchase the item, the author will receive an affiliate commission. Regardless, I only recommend products or services I use personally and believe will add value to my readers. I am disclosing this in accordance with the Federal Trade Commission's 16 CFR, Part 255: "Guides Concerning the Use of Endorsements and Testimonials in Advertising."

ISBN-10: 1523376007
ISBN-13: 978-1523376001

DEDICATION

This book is for the busy and the overworked. The professional who is desperately eager to make a change in their life; the aspiring entrepreneur who can see the writing on the wall and who has the taste of freedom in their mouth, and who is looking for the strategy to help them make an exit on their terms.

But, most of all, this book is for my wife, Ashley, who stood by me, encouraged me, and walked beside me every step of the way.

CONTENTS

Receive exclusive updates and become an official Strategist!

Get the most out of *Exit Strategy* and share your success story with the community by visiting

www.theexitstrategybook.com/join

EXIT STRATEGY

A master in the art of living draws no sharp distinction between his work and his play; his labor and his leisure; his mind and his body; his education and his recreation. He hardly knows which is which. He simply pursues his vision of excellence through whatever he is doing and leaves others to determine whether he is working or playing. To himself, he always appears to be doing both.
- L.P. Jacks

INTRODUCTION

I'm not one of those entrepreneurs who gave up their six-figure salary and fancy office to start a business, and I wasn't selling lemonade to my neighbors when I was seven. I was not born an entrepreneur, and I never laid awake at night dreaming of owning my own business.

I was forced to make a decision. In 2014, I had to decide if I'd try and make it work as an entrepreneur or if I would send out resumes and attempt to find another job. I'm an average guy who has been blessed to be able to do amazing things with incredible people. I started where you are now. In the beginning, I knew little about starting a business, but I found a way to make it work. Rather, I'm *finding* a way to make it work a little more each day.

Almost twelve months to the day after I received the highest award my sales department could offer, I was put on a performance improvement plan. Eleven months after that, and just three months after earning the highest achievement award on my sales team for my territory, I was fired.

I learned the hard way that everyone is expendable. I went from being recognized as the most successful salesperson in a business unit that generated $2 billion a year in revenue, to being put on an "improvement" plan in just twelve months. And, I made the transition from the team rock star to the team pariah in sixty days. I've learned my lesson, and I learned it the hardest way possible.

The lesson is this: even the founder of the company can be dismissed if they aren't performing the way the decision-makers think they should. Don't believe me? Just ask the Steve Jobs of the early 1980s. Just nine years after launching Apple Computer from his family's garage, Jobs was voted out of the company by its board members and the CEO.

Unless you're in the position of power, you're expendable. I learned it when I was fired by a guy who used to be my friend; Steve Jobs learned it when he was fired from the company he started, and I hope you never have to learn it. All we're able to rely on is our ability to perform. Once your performance is put into question, your time is short.

However, this book isn't about getting fired. It's not about getting kicked out of your job or being asked to leave your company. This book is about possibilities. It's about the future and your place in it. This book is about taking back control of your life, betting on yourself, and developing a strategy to make the transition to entrepreneurship.

At this point, you could think to yourself, "This book won't work for me," and walk away. However, if you do, you'll likely always wonder what could have happened if you bet on yourself and took a chance. Please, don't put yourself in a position down the road where you look back at your life and ask, *"What if I'd read* Exit Strategy *and did everything it said? How could things be different for my family and me?"*

This book is here to help you develop your exit strategy. Together we'll put together a plan to help you make the transition from corporate outsider to entrepreneurial master. I'll show you what it took me years to realize and only minutes to fully understand.

I'll share my story with you. The ups, downs, achievements and mistakes, so you can see that we're a lot alike, if not *just* alike.

If this book does its job, we'll not only get to know one another as kindred spirits, but we'll take a journey together that will change both of our lives. Together we'll develop an exit strategy that will help you leave your job behind, live the life you were meant to live, and help you make a difference in the world by using your strengths and doing what makes you happy.

We'll examine strategy - the overall philosophy, mindset requirements, and beliefs that will help you become successful. Your strategy will be the battle plan that will shape your tactics - the day to day activities, tasks, and actions that will move you forward.

Instead of throwing spaghetti at the wall and waiting around to see what's left the next day, we'll put together a plan to help you move forward, so you never have to go back to a job again. No more working somewhere you are miserable. No more reporting for duty to a boss that couldn't care less whether you're sick, your family member is in the hospital, or if you just need a freakin' break.

If you're ready, I'm ready. But, before we move forward, I must ask you a question, and I feel like I should warn you.

Why are you here?

Why did you pick up this book off the shelf? Why did you decide to open it and start reading?

What is that deep, driving force that is motivating you to live with passion, escape a place of misery, or try something new?

For some people, it's their children - parents who realize they're not setting the example they'd like to for their kids who see them coming home from work in a bad mood every day.

For others, it's the pull to strike out on their own and live life on the edge. They want to work from the mountain tops or the beach; it doesn't matter so long as they're not stuck in an office.

For me, if I were in your position, it would be the desire not to feel sick to my stomach every time I walked into my office or like I wanted to die every time I logged into my corporate computer. I would want to enjoy life again, to be happy, and to not be a miserable sonofabitch around my family and friends because I was so unhappy at work.

Whatever the reason, I want you to think about it for a moment and keep thinking about this driving motivation as you continue reading this book. Your future will depend on your ability to stay focused and moving forward as challenges arise.

I'm here with you, and you can always email me at ellory@ellorywells.com if you need a little support.

Better yet, why not take five minutes *right now,* and email me what motivates you and keeps you moving forward. That way, when times get tough, you can look back at that email and remember what it's like to be in a spot you don't enjoy and how sweet it will be when you're finally doing something you enjoy.

And now my warning.

This book is a no holds barred look at the workplace today. I'm going to be honest and tell things as I see them. And, I'm going to share things with you that you might not like. There's no other way for you and me to move forward if we can't trust each other. Together, we can do this. With the right planning and dedication to your future, you can do anything you want. I believe in you. And, I never want you to go back to a job you hate or report to a boss who doesn't have your best interest at heart ever again.

This book is for you.

This book is your exit strategy.

FOREWARD

Before you spend the next few hours, days, or weeks reading and studying this book, I want to take a brief moment and share why I decided to write it. If I can help you either invest your time wisely or save you some of the finite amount of time you have on this earth, I can feel like I've helped you.

Over my years of study, I've found no shortage of literature advising the career-minded about how to climb-the-corporate-ladder. I've also found plenty of books on leadership and entrepreneurship.

However, I've found few (if any) books on helping you develop and deploy an exit strategy that will help you leave your day job and build a business of your own. I've never found a book that shares techniques that will help you find your first customer, develop business systems that will help you automate and scale, or how to think like a business owner.

I wrote this book to show you how to do those things. Because, how to find clients, how to manage systems and hire contract workers are the types of things my coaching and mastermind clients want to know. They're the strategies and tactics all aspiring entrepreneurs are looking for.

Instead of theory, I want to give you action items. Instead of helping you grow your business from $10,000 to $100,000 a year,

I want to help you formulate a plan to leave where you *have* to be and transition to where you *want* to be.

I want you to tell a story that is uniquely yours, and live your life with purpose, passion, and, of course, profit.

In Part I of *Exit Strategy,* I invite you to walk with me through some of the moments that have shaped who I am over the past few years. I'm not a larger than life celebrity, and I've experienced no extraordinary circumstances that have helped me achieve my goals. I don't possess some particular talent that you don't have.

You'll see throughout this book and especially in Part I, that I'm not special except for the fact that I have the ability to focus, analyze and then simplify better than anyone else I know. Those skills, however, were learned over time, and they coincide with some of my core strengths. The skills and strengths you possess, even if you don't yet know what they are, will be two of the things that make you successful.

In Part II, you'll want to refill your coffee cup and get a fresh pen or highlighter because this is where we really get to work. We'll look at tactical things most teachers don't go into much detail about. I will show you the tactics of not only what to do, but how to do it and what tools you could use. You'll learn how to get more traffic to your website or business, convert visitors and foot traffic into subscribers and customers, how to create content that sells, and much more. Every great business is built upon a solid foundation, and Part II is where you'll build or strengthen yours.

In Part III, we'll build on everything you've learned so far and we'll put it into a timeline that would have aided me greatly had I had it when I began. I've studied my successes and failures over the past several years, and I've pulled out the parts that worked, distilled the lessons from the things that didn't, and crafted the Roadmap you'll find in Part III. Had I the ability to re-write history, this is how I'd write it.

Part IV is where everything we've discussed, and all the work you put in during the Roadmap in Part III, comes together toward your long term success.

To be honest, it's during the activities of Part IV when most people decide to throw in the towel and quit. They discover that being an entrepreneur, starting a business, betting on yourself, and creating their own success is a lot of work. And, for some, it's more work than they're willing to do. Building a business, a legacy if you will, is something that takes a monumental amount of time and effort. And, instead of standing up, stretching, and grabbing an energy drink and a snack, they decide to settle.

Don't settle.

Be bold.

Stay strong.

Also in Part IV, you'll meet my friends Dale, Tamara, and John - real life entrepreneurs who are out there making money, working with clients, and growing their businesses. You'll get to read their stories, learn how they signed their first clients, and discover how they launched their businesses. I think you'll really enjoy reading about them, and I'm excited to be able to share each of their stories with you.

Last, in Part V, you'll find my recommended reading list of books that have changed my life. I've studied each of these books, and they helped shape who I am. More practically, these works also provided the guidance I needed to create business plans, develop products, and embrace the mindset necessary for becoming an entrepreneur.

Additionally, you'll find the list of tools and resources I've mentioned throughout the book and which have helped me start and grow my online business. With one exception, I have used each tool myself and have thoroughly tested them in a live production environment. You'll find many of these tools in use on my sites, and I wouldn't recommend them if I didn't believe they'd help you. Are you ready? Let's go!

PART I - WE'RE IN THIS TOGETHER

A rising tide doesn't raise people who don't have a boat.
We have to build the boat for them. We have to give them
the basic infrastructure to rise with the tide.
- Rahul Gandhi

My goal with Part I of this book is to show you that anything I've done you can do too. You and I are alike. I was not born an entrepreneur, I didn't get special training, and I didn't have any connections with "A-listers" who helped get me going.

We're in this together. If you can use this book to develop your exit strategy and make the transition from a job you hate to work you love, we both win.

The better you do, the better I'll do, and vice versa. The game of life and entrepreneurship isn't zero sum - if one of us wins, it doesn't mean the other has to lose. Your successes don't cancel out mine. As your build your business, remember:

The rising tide raises all boats.

When you succeed, we all succeed. When you do better, we all do better. We need each other if any of us is going to survive and thrive in business. We're in this together.

1: DOING EVERYTHING RIGHT

There are a lot of things that are personally uncomfortable to show, especially me without makeup and completely bloated or crying. But I've realized that it's time for me to show my audience that you don't have to be perfect to achieve your dreams. Because nobody relates to being perfect.
- Katy Perry

I've done several stupid things in my life. Some of those things even happened while I was at work. One time, I got so frustrated and annoyed that I mimicked stabbing a zebra print couch with my pocket knife while in the break room (I've never told that story before). Ya, stupid stuff.

But in 2008, I was abiding by all of the rules. Like many people during the demise of the American economy in the late 2000s, I was doing everything right, and it still wasn't enough.

But my story doesn't begin there. It started in December of 2006, when I walked across the stage in Waco, Texas to receive my Bachelor of Arts degree in Psychology from Baylor University. I'd taken an extra "half-lap" and finished my degree in four and a half years. I was glad to be done with school and eager to start making some real money to support my video game habit.

After graduation, I bounced from job to job. I hauled flowers, trees, and shrubs at a nursery, tried to sell obnoxious zebra-print furniture, and even worked in a retail store selling cigars. Looking back at that time in my life, I realize how much I was begging to win the approval of others. I desperately wanted to find someone who would pay me to make money for them. I was hoping someone would allow me to earn money for them, help them build their business, and live the life they wanted to live.

Silly.

Finally, in the summer of 2008, I made the connection I was looking for. Through the friend of a friend (aka my network), I was able to snag an interview at IBM in Dallas, Texas. If I played my cards right, I could go from fertilizer and heat to computers and A/C.

After three rounds of interviews, I finally got the call I'd been waiting for. The hiring manager said he wanted to take me out to a Texas Rangers baseball game and talk. After drinking a little too much over-priced beer and enjoying the game, my future employer told me to expect a call from the HR department the next day. He also advised me that I should ask for $1000 more than what I was going to be offered and that I'd most likely get it.

When it was all said and done, I'd successfully made the transition from $12.50 an hour to a salary of $50,000 a year. Things were good.

After getting my first month's paychecks, I moved out of a bedroom in my dad's house into a two bed, two bath apartment in the Valley Ranch area of Irving, Texas, across from where the Dallas Cowboys had their practice facility. Toward the end of 2007, things were finally looking up after a year and a half of job hopping and trying to work my way up the ladder at an investment company where nobody wanted to talk to a young, twenty-something kid about investing money when the financial world was crumbling. At the time, if the conversation didn't have to do with how far under the mattress to shove your cash, a discussion about smart money planning wasn't on anybody's radar.

About two weeks into my new job at IBM, my boss realized I didn't know as much about their technology as he thought I knew. I hadn't lied in the interviews, but I wasn't as knowledgeable about IBM's products and services as they would have liked.

I remember sitting in his corner cubicle. We had one of our weekly meetings, and he asked me,

"Ellory, how would you explain the differences between X and P?"

I had no idea what he was talking about. I thought he was taking me back to algebra or geometry, and I was as clueless in that cubicle as I was in 10th grade.

After that brief meeting to assess my knowledge, I was found wanting and reassigned to a four-month training program to remedy my ignorance. As it turns out, X and P were two of the most popular models of IBM servers that I should have been familiar with.

Oops.

For the next several months, I did everything right. I did what I was told, showed up where I was supposed to be, and learned with the best of them. I excelled at all parts of the training. I led teams, participated like a champ, and networked with the other trainees after hours. I not only learned about IBM's culture but about how to sell and determine customer needs. I learned how to uncover problems and figure out solutions. One thing I didn't do so well was stay in touch with the team I was hired to join. Had I done that better, things might have turned out differently.

One afternoon, the other trainees and I were called into a large conference room for a training session. It was during this exercise that I first learned about the DWYSYWD principle. DWYSYWD is an acronym that stands for Do What You Say You Will Do, and it was to be the basis for how to interact with our clients, with each other, and with the company if we were going to be successful.

That strategy is one I still deploy today. In fact, "dwizzy-wid," how you'd pronounce the acronym and palindrome D-W-Y-S-Y-W-D, is what I decided to name my business several years later.

My corporate education continued, and a scorching summer turned into mild winter. I saved money, paid off most of my debts, started furnishing my new apartment, and began to enjoy and embrace the yuppie lifestyle. As the year rolled over into 2009, I was optimistic about what the future would bring.

However, my optimism wouldn't last long. By the end of the first month of the year, I'd have begun to change my world view, and I'd experience something I hope you never have to go through yourself. Every plan I had made for my future would be put on hold, and I'd learn a life lesson that would shape who I am, how I would see the world and do business far into the future.

In January of 2009, my world got rocked.

2: LIFE ON HOLD

And it's a human need to be told stories. The more we're governed by idiots and have no control over our destinies, the more we need to tell stories to each other about who we are, why we are, where we come from, and what might be possible.
- Alan Rickman

U p until this point in my life, that is until 2009, I believed that doing what your bosses told you to do translated into job security. If you did what you were supposed to, and you did it well enough while keeping a low profile, you would be able to make it safely to retirement.

Even typing that paragraph feels ridiculous. Who wants to work for forty years and look back and say "I kept my head down, did what I was told and didn't make any waves"?

But, that's what I naively thought. And how most people still think. However, nothing could be further from the truth as you're about to see.

On June 28th, 2002 in Waco, Texas, I met the girl who would one day become my wife. On the intramural soccer fields of the "Fountain Mall" on Baylor's campus after a long day of Freshman orientation, I gave up my snow cone so Ashley could have it, and our friendship began.

For the remainder of the summer, before we moved into the freshman dorms, Ashley and I stayed in touch, chatting via AIM during the day and over the phone at night. We dated on and off (mostly on) throughout college. She studied biology, and I focused on psychology.

But, we're getting ahead of ourselves.

Friday

In January 2009, after almost seven years of friendship, I decided it was finally time to propose. Ashley and I would be the last of our college friends to get married, and it was time to move our lives forward together.

One Friday morning, I got up the courage to drive to Robbins Brothers in Dallas to go engagement ring shopping. After what seemed like hours of looking at things I couldn't afford, I finally found a ring that was the right cut, clarity, color, and carat, and most importantly, it was one that I could afford. The white gold band held the princess cut diamond perfectly.

However, I couldn't afford the entire price of the ring. I could only pay for part of it, so I had the salesperson put the ring on layaway, and I paid what I could. I left the store and headed back to work nervous but still feeling like a badass.

Monday

The following Monday, rumors started to circulate that major layoffs were coming. At the time, I doubt I was familiar with what layoffs meant for the company, and I certainly had no idea what kind of emotional (and financial) toll being laid off could have on a family.

In my naivety, I assumed I was safe from the Corporate purge. Since I'd only been at IBM for a few months, I figured they'd keep me around. After all, they'd just spent over $40,000 paying me to learn sales techniques, pipeline management, and communication and negotiation skills, not to mention the history and beliefs of the company. I thought I'd be safe given the fact that they'd just sent me through a very expensive corporate education.

I was wrong.

The next day I went to work, and it was business as usual. Everything seemed fine; the only difference was that the layoff rumors were no longer rumors. Colleagues were getting their pink slips and being sent home all over the building and all across the company.

Wednesday

On Wednesday morning, just like dozens of Wednesdays before it, I went to work thinking I was safe. I was carefree as I walked into the training room to have coffee with my fellow new employees who were mostly recent college and MBA graduates.

Everything seemed fine until the first member of our training class was called into a meeting with James, the head of human resources. The rest of us waited intently as the clock ticked by, each click of the minute hand counting down to the unknown.

About seven minutes later our friend returned. Everything was okay. Phew! We were all so relieved to know that the brief meeting was just HR's way of letting us know what was going on and to let us know we were safe because we were in training.

And so the day went. One new hire would return, and the next person would get called to head to the small conference room in the middle of the building. Each person came back with the same message - all is well.

Then 4:15 rolled around, and it was my turn. With a smile on my face and not a care in the world, I walked over to the small, windowless room and sat down in an office chair almost knee to knee with the same human resources manager who I'd negotiated with just months earlier for an extra $1000 a year.

"Hi Ellory, how are you doing today?" he said.

"I'm fine, thank you" I replied.

"I'm sure you've heard about the recent resource actions that have been going on this week?"

"Yes, I have."

"Well, unfortunately, Ellory, you've been affected by the resource action and…" he said without emotion.

I don't remember much after that. It's weird; as clear as I remember the first thirty seconds of that meeting, I have no memory of what happened after that or how long I was in the room. Most of the meetings with my friends had lasted just a few minutes, but I could have been in there for hours, I have no idea.

3: THE NEXT 30 DAYS

You must take personal responsibility. You cannot change
the circumstances, the seasons, or the wind, but you can
change yourself. That is something you have charge of.
- Jim Rohn

After that meeting on Wednesday, everything changed for me. I realized that even though I had done everything right, done everything I was told to do (and had done it really well), I was still expendable. I had excelled at the training, led the class in many ways, and had prepared myself for future success on the sales floor, but it still wasn't enough.

Though I was fairly bitter, I later realized I couldn't blame the company. As hard as the situation was, I couldn't get around the fact that they'd hired me to do a job I wasn't doing.

I told you I was going to be brutally honest, didn't I.

IBM gave every other employee "affected by the resource action" and me a month to find another job within the company. So, for the next twenty days, I networked, drank coffee with hiring managers, continued to wear a tie and dress pants, and submitted dozens of resumes to anyone who I thought could possibly hire me. During the last ten days of my final month with the company, I began to lose steam. I was less enthusiastic, less optimistic, and my search efforts began to show signs of wariness.

At the end of February 2009, I turned in my badge, said my goodbyes, and headed back to my two bedroom, two bathroom apartment across from the Cowboys' practice camp.

Knowing my tiny severance check wouldn't last long, I packed up my stuff from the apartment I'd rented with pride just months before, and moved to a one bedroom studio apartment at the bottom of the hill and continued my search.

During the months that followed, I re-watched every movie I owned and proceeded to re-play every video game regardless of whether I'd beaten them before or not. I remember playing hours of Halo online with my friends and feeling both frustrated and exhausted by the job search.

It went on that way for three months. I applied for jobs and made no progress. While I was young, eager, well-educated and had a decent resume, I was competing against people with years, even decades, more experience than me.

Looking back, I realize how demeaning the job search can be. Why is it that we're satisfied running around begging anybody with a pulse and a bank account to hire us? When did we start believing that the only way to make a living was to give up control to someone else? How did that become acceptable?

I get it. I do. From a young age, we're told to sit down, be quite, don't run, raise your hand, stand in line, take your test, finish your breakfast, be on time, tie your shoes and don't talk to strangers. And, if we don't follow every rule all the time we get in trouble.

It took me three months to find someone willing to hire me and pay me half of what I was making before. I went from a career with a future (or so I thought) and making $50,000 to a job I started to dislike immediately for $26,000.

In May of 2009, I was no longer unemployed, but I found myself doing something I didn't enjoy. I sucked it up, did what I was told, and felt grateful for the opportunity.

4: THANK YOU SIR, MAY I HAVE ANOTHER

I believe that if life gives you lemons, you should make lemonade... And try to find somebody whose life has given them vodka, and have a party.
- Ron White

You may be wondering why I'm sharing these details about my life. You may even be thinking to yourself, "Wow, Ellory sure is an ungrateful s-o-b." Well no, I'm not ungrateful. But, we'll get to that.

The reason I'm sharing my story is that each of these experiences taught me something and has helped shaped who I am and how I see the world. Every time I share parts of my journey, whether it's from the stage at a conference or over a cup of coffee at my weekly meetup spot, some part of my story connects with someone. Whenever I think I've shared too much, it's not long afterward that a new friend tells me how they had a similar experience.

If I skip the details, maybe a tiny one I thought about passing over, I miss a chance to connect with you. And, if not you, the person who read this book before or after you.

As they say, the devil is in the details, and everyone loves a good story.

***

After my three months of unemployment, I got a job selling advertising space to companies in New Jersey. And, when I say "advertising space" I really mean spots in the yellow pages. The company who hired me handled the business directory listings for Verizon, and my territory happened to be the northeast part of the United States.

Once they'd thoroughly trained us in the art of matching coded skus to their ads in corresponding sizes and shapes, and whether those ads had color or if they were simply black and white, we graduated to the sales floor. Every two weeks we'd get a new ten-page list of companies to call. Every two weeks we'd get a new territory and leave the old one behind. Every two weeks we'd start over cold calling businesses and trying to make new contacts.

While at that job I heard it all. Sales reps pushing the truth to get what they want, verbal harassment and often outright lies. I shared a cubicle wall with an older man who had audible gas every afternoon and the stereotypical loud-mouthed salesperson who would try every trick in the book to make a sale.

I know I shouldn't have, but I regularly reminisced about the old days working for "Big Blue." It's human nature to take things for granted, and I was no exception. I'd felt pride in working for IBM. I felt like it made me better than other people because of the prestige of the company. But, here I was, with those other people doing the same things for the same kind of money.

5: A LIGHT AT THE END OF THE TUNNEL

Progress is impossible without change, and those who cannot change their minds cannot change anything.
- ***George Bernard Shaw***

Though I had a job that paid the bills, I wasn't satisfied. On one hand, it's always good to be on the lookout for the next big thing. If Alexander Graham Bell hadn't felt that way, he might not have ever invented the telephone. If Elon Musk hadn't dedicated his life to the next big thing, electric cars might never have become commonplace. On the other hand, never being satisfied and always searching for an upgrade can be a bad thing, especially if you're married.

Well, I wasn't married, at least not yet. Remember that engagement ring I mentioned before? Ya, that one. It was still sitting in a Robbins Brothers storage locker under lock and key on layaway.

For three months I tried my hardest to sell ad space on a dying medium. Had I known then what I know now, I could have made a killing selling websites to these companies instead of quarter-page ads. Instead of building someone else's business as an employee, I could have been constructing mine as the owner.

One day I decided to reach out to an old manager contact. Emily had been my manager when I worked for Dell back in college and through the power of the internet, I knew she still worked there. With little to lose, I emailed her out of desperation and asked if there were any job opportunities she could connect me to.

As luck would have it, there was. I drove down to Round Rock one scorching summer day and had an awkward interview with Tim and Chris.

Unlike my experience at IBM where I knew little about the hardware, I was a virtual expert on Dell equipment which I'd sold in college while working at the Baylor Computer Store. I knew how to sell, and I knew the technology. This job would be perfect.

That is if I didn't screw it up. Which I almost did, even before my first day.

As the interview with Tim and Chris drew to a close, I began to get comfortable. Actually, a little too comfortable. Both managers knew I'd driven down for the day, and I was about to make the three-hour drive back up to Dallas. Throughout the interview, the three of us had talked about traffic, they could see where I was working and living currently, and they knew how I'd been introduced to them through Emily.

As we were wrapping up, Chris looked me in the eye and asked me the question that almost cost me the job.

"So, do you plan on relocating if you get the position?" He asked.

And, without missing a beat, I replied, "Nope, I'll be commuting."

If you've ever met me in person, you may have picked up on the fact that I have a dry sense of humor. Like Seinfeld, I regularly deliver my comedic wit with a straight face. I later learned that this type of comedy is commonly referred to as "deadpan."

My smart-ass response delivered with nary a grin in sight almost cost me over $200,000. I later found out that, because of my misunderstood comment, Chris didn't want Tim to hire me and even tried to prevent him from doing it.

Well, screw you, Chris. You can borrow my Sales Rep of the Year trophy and Team Rockstar trophy and have a Seinfeld rerun watching party on Hulu Plus.

Needless to say, Tim made the right choice and hired me against the desperate and misguided urgings of Chris. With the new job offer in hand, everything started to change for the better.

6: BACK ON TRACK

The key to success is to focus our conscious mind on things we desire, not things we fear.
- Brian Tracy

A s soon as I received the official job offer from Dell, I turned in my two-week notice to my manager at the yellow page ad company. I couldn't get out of there fast enough.

There was one great thing, however, that did come out of that job. After downsizing my apartment and cutting entertainment back to almost nil, I was able to save up enough money to finally get Ashley's engagement ring out of layaway.

I can still remember walking into Robbins Brothers and fanning a dozen hundred dollar bills out on the table. I thought I was so cool, and I was. Name another time in life when you can pay cash for expensive jewelry and fan a week's worth of your time and effort out on a table. I can't think of any.

The day before my birthday, Ashley and I drove to our friends' house near McKinney. Ashley's friend, Kristin, was the only one in on the secret, and that night I popped the question in front of our closest friends. The ring I'd picked out seven months before, back when I was happy and ignorant while working at IBM, was now finally where it belonged, on Ashley's finger.

I moved to Round Rock to pursue my career at Dell and Ashley joined me a few months later after we got married on a beach in Florida. Finally, everything was coming together and going according to plan.

7: ACCORDING TO PLAN

Plans are nothing; planning is everything.
- Dwight D. Eisenhower

The next few years proceeded according to almost any plan ever written for newlyweds. Everything went perfectly. Ashley and I rented a great apartment, we adopted a cat and began building a beautiful two-story house on the golf course a few months later.

By the time Ashley and I'd been married a year, we'd moved into our new home, she'd applied to go back to school, and things were going well for me at work.

For the next two and half years, everything was great. I was getting to travel for work, I earned a 3.4% raise (twice!), and I saw opportunities for growth within the company.

Then things started to change. As with most falls from paradise, there was no major catastrophe that left everyone screaming in panic. The change happened slowly, one step at a time.

At first, we began to notice that our parties were getting smaller. I know what you're thinking, "Woopty-do, cry me a river, no parties?" But you don't understand; Dell was a successful tech company in the late 2000s when technology and the internet were growing dramatically. We had vendor money to burn.

To put things in perspective, the first Christmas party I went to in 2009 cost over $75,000. Spouses were invited, and there were hundreds of people in the ballroom of the Marriott hotel. Included in that $75,000 budget was over $40,000 in prizes ranging from $300 laptops to $5000 travel vouchers. Food and alcohol were included, and it was a grand "wow" event that welcomed me to the company.

Fast forward four years, and we got $50 gift cards to Target.

For the first two years I was there, Dell had been insulated from the failing economy. However, that was changing. New management was brought in (you know how that goes), and hiring freezes were put into place all over the company. My prospects for advancement were dwindling, and the mood over the department was starting to slip.

Back when I worked as the sous chef at Sonic when I was sixteen, I learned a lesson. If you weren't busy, you were sent home. Then, as the fashion designer at American Eagle when I was seventeen, I learned that if you didn't have something to do, you were sent home. Then, as the head landscape artist at Calloway's Nursery at twenty-four, I was a pro and always had a broom in my hand or a plant that needed potting.

In reality, I flipped burgers and made shakes, straightened and folded clothes, and hauled fertilizer and watered thirsty trees. Even if the jobs weren't as glamorous as I would have liked, they still taught me a valuable lesson: create value or go home.

So, when things started to go south at Dell, I remembered the lessons I'd learned while mopping floors and straightening the fall line of jeans. I began working on myself and went looking for things to do. I started reading personal development books

8: THE BEGINNING OF THE END

Don't wait. The time will never be just right.
- Napoleon Hill

I f you don't listen to podcasts, you should; radio these days is awful. There's a podcast out there by Michael O'Neal that's worth listening to called *The Solopreneur Hour*.[1] The tagline for his show is, "Job security for the unemployable."

And that's what I was becoming, unemployable. As I began to read and work on myself, I was becoming less of the ideal employee and more of the aspiring entrepreneur. In the fall of 2011, without knowing it, I set in motion things that would have devastating effects on my career, livelihood, and even my marriage.

What was this awful thing? What did I do that would end up getting me fired from my career doing something I loved and was great at? What could have caused all of the emotional pain and mental anguish that I would eventually put my wife and me through?

I read a book.

---

[1] You can find The Solopreneur Hour Podcast at http://www.solopreneurhour.com

I'm not sure how I heard about this particular book, but I picked up and read an old copy of *The Flight of the Buffalo: Soaring to Excellence, Learning to Let Employees Lead* by James A. Belasco and Ralph C. Stayer. Reading that book was the beginning of the end for me. I learned so much about doing business, taking and placing responsibility on the people who were responsible, and how to lead others.

After that, I was hooked. I couldn't get enough personal development and the more I read, the more I wanted. However, the more I read, the worse things became at work. The more I read, and the more I learned, the more unemployable I became. To see my recommended reading list, please refer to Appendix A at the end of the book, or at www.theexitstrategybook.com/appendix-a/.

I read everything I could get my hands on. Over the next twelve months, I would go on to read over twenty books on leadership, personal branding, self-help, sales, and mindset training. I was hungry for knowledge and the more books I consumed, the more books I bought. I think I single-handedly kept the local Half Price Books in business.

And, the more I read about leadership and business, the more my eyes were opened to what was going on around me. I began to see things I'd never seen before. What I thought was business as usual, and "just how large companies operate" I started to see as poor leadership and inadequate management.

Every book I read showed me a glimpse at a better future; a way things could be if company leadership would only read the same things I was reading.

So, I did the only sensible thing. I started a book club.

Taking the famous Gandhi quote to heart, I decided to be the change I wanted to see in my department. I wanted to take initiative and demonstrate my leadership skills. I thought I was doing the right thing by putting an emphasis on personal development within the company. If I wanted the work environment to change, I would be the catalyst it needed, and I would start a movement amongst my peers to do the same.

So that I wouldn't take valuable time away from the business, I held my book club meetings during the lunch hour in a conference room down the hall. When I pitched my book club idea to our Executive Director, he was in full support, and I got approval to email the entire department about the meeting. I received a fair amount of interest, and at first, everything looked good. At first.

If I'm perfectly honest, and I told you I would be, I started the book club because I thought it might help me get promoted. I wanted to move up in the company. At the time, starting a book club focused on making my teammates and I better seemed like a good idea and an excellent way to stand out from the crowd.

Right out of the gate I started messing up. The club's inaugural book was *The 21 Irrefutable Laws of Leadership* by John Maxwell. Right away my peers began to see the things I had started noticing months before and I had to work hard every week to keep our meetings from turning into a gripe session about management.

Let me give you an example. Growing up, my wife's dad always grilled his steaks to well done. She was raised thinking that gray with ketchup was how you were supposed to eat it. Fast forward a dozen or so years and I take her to a steakhouse and order my sirloin with a hot, red center, juicy and delicious. After she had gotten over the shock of seeing how a steak should be cooked, her eyes were opened to a whole new world of delicious culinary cuisine. Once she tasted what she was missing she could never go back to gray meat again.

My book club was for my coworkers like that medium-rare steak was for Ashley. Once they saw what was possible, they couldn't ignore the way things had been, and they definitely couldn't go back.

While *Flight of the Buffalo* was the beginning of the end, my book club was the smaller rock that smacked the slightly larger rock and knocked it over the edge and down the hill.

Over the next several months my book club read many more books. Jeff Olson taught us in *The Slight Edge* that we never get anywhere by accident; that we get where we are by taking small actions and repeating them over time.

When we read *Good to Great* by Jim Collins, we learned about teamwork and surrounding ourselves with the right people. Collins told us how focused leaders could change the course of a company's history and make changes for the better.

In *Drive*, Daniel Pink showed us that not all salespeople are coin-operated like our managers told us. He put into words what we were feeling about wanting something more than money to be a motivating factor. We learned that people with purpose are not only happier at work, but that they perform better too. Pink showed us that what drives us isn't dollars but the pursuit of excellence, the quest for conquering a challenge, and the pursuit of our passion.

These books and several more showed us what we were missing. They gave us a glimpse of what Corporate America was leaving out. The authors of these books connected with us in a way that our managers never could and never seemed to want to.

I didn't realize it at the time, but I was hurtling toward the point of no return. I was changing on the inside and becoming unredeemable.

9: JOHN MAXWELL RUINS MY CAREER AND THE POINT OF NO RETURN

The point of no return is the point beyond which one must continue on one's current course of action because turning back is physically impossible, prohibitively expensive, or dangerous.
- Wikipedia

In every relationship there's always a point of no return; a place in time at which you can no longer go back to the way things were. Sometimes that point is a devastating injury or a moment of indiscretion, something you can't un-see or undo. At other times, like when you meet that special someone, you fall head over heels and are no longer able to see her as "just a friend." For me, it was nothing like that. For me, the point of no return was that very first book we read as a book club, *The 21 Irrefutable Laws of Leadership.*

Even though I'd read dozens of books on business and leadership at this point, I was still skeptical about the lessons they taught. I can remember thinking to myself, "Okay, that's fantastic for small companies, but I still don't know if these principles can scale to a business with 100,000 employees." Everything I'd read up until this point talked directly to the small and medium business owner and used examples of business with far fewer employees than the companies I had experience with.

But, when I read Maxwell's famous book, everything changed. In Chapter 5, The Law of Addition, Maxwell tells the story of Costco co-founder and then CEO, Jim Sinegal. To put things in perspective, as of 2014 Costco was the third largest retailer in the United States, and in 2015, they were listed as the second largest in the world. Costco owns over 670 warehouse locations and employs over 180,000 people all over the globe.[2]

It could go without saying, but I'll say it anyway: my theory that great leadership principles and the idea of putting people first and paying them more might not scale to large companies was entirely disproved. If Sinegal, who led one of the biggest businesses in the world could do business a better way, so could the managers, directors and vice presidents at Dell.

When I finished *21 Laws,* I decided I could never view my company's leadership the same way again. I could never again be satisfied with management who put people last and took credit for the work of others. No longer could I stomach what I saw going on around me.

And, apparently, no longer could I keep my big mouth shut.

---

[2]Wikipedia - https://en.wikipedia.org/wiki/Costco

10: CIRCLING THE DRAIN

Thinking will not overcome fear but action will.
- W. Clement Stone

O nce the cat was out of the bag, she was never going back in again. It's like the amazing magic trick after you finally find out the secret; there's nothing magical about it. After discovering that better things did exist, and a better alternative was out there, I couldn't go back.

Over the last few years, I've started saying that personal development books should come with a warning label, "CAUTION: Reading this book could be hazardous to your career!"

From that point forward, management couldn't do anything right. It's not like they tried particularly hard, but I was always on the lookout for what they could have done better. As I read more books, the problems showed up with increasing frequency.

I maintained my focus on personal development. I continued to host the book club meetings and quell the inevitable peasant uprisings they encouraged. And, I continued to write on my blog which I'll share more about later.

Over the next several months, book club attendance began to dwindle. Very few people prioritize their personal development, and that's why very few people ever become successful. To make sure I was always there, I would block off time on my calendar both before and after my book club meetings so no one could schedule something during *my* time.

If you don't prioritize what *you* want to accomplish, other people will make plans for you, and they'll prioritize what *they* want to accomplish. Setting time aside to do what you want to do is one thing every successful person does well. Successful people own their calendars instead of being slaves to them. You either own your calendar, or it will own you.

I owned my calendar and was very successful as a salesperson at Dell. I took what I learned from the book club and applied those lessons to selling and leading a team. Even when no one else showed up for the meeting (yes, that happened more than once), I'd still take the time out of my day and read. That time alone and away from the sales floor helped me focus on what was important and figure out how to navigate the waters of Corporate America.

This went on for almost a year. We'd choose a new book to read as a group, and fewer people would show up each week. We didn't have a large group to begin with, so it wasn't long before I was the only one left. I soon stopped adding the meetings to the calendar or asking people why they didn't show.

Soon, as the number of people at work whom I could talk to started to disappear, I decided to take to the internet. As any self-respecting individual with an abundance of opinion would do; I started a blog.

11: THE COFFIN AND THE NAIL

The future is something which everyone reaches at the rate of 60 minutes an hour, whatever he does, whoever he is.
- C. S. Lewis

There are several points along the timeline of my story where I can see things changing. Each book I read was another strike of the hammer driving a wedge between where I was and where I wanted to be. Each blog post I wrote on my website was another nail being driven into the coffin of my career, getting ever closer to sealing my fate.

In January of 2012, I started sharing the things I was learning with colleagues both inside and outside of the company. What began as a casual conversation among my teammates who I shared a cubicle wall with soon turned into a document I would send out to about a dozen people across the country.

In addition to reading books, I also spent a good deal of time reading blogs and news articles. I browsed *Entrepreneur, Inc., Business Insider*, the *Harvard Business Review*, the *Wall Street Journal*, and many other online publications. If I found an article I enjoyed and thought would help or inspire someone else, I'd provide a fifty-word summary and a link and add the post to the weekly newsletter. I'd compile favorite reads, save the document as a PDF, and send it to people who I thought would like it.

After the second time I did this, I received a call from my friend Kevin who I had met at IBM a few years before. He and I had stayed in touch, and if it weren't for his phone call, I wouldn't be where I am today.

Kevin didn't give me any advice or offer any wisdom. He only mentioned that my weekly newsletter had inspired him to do more than he was doing and start living with more purpose. He wanted to leave a legacy and be remembered for having a positive impact on the world.

My inspiration of Kevin and him telling me about it, in turn, inspired me. The very next day, on Saturday, January 28th, I started my first blog.

In the beginning, I knew nothing about blogging. In fact, I didn't want to call my site a blog. Instead, I insisted on calling it a website. I didn't call my weekly writing "blog posts," I insisted on calling them "articles." I thought blogging was for sixteen-year-old girls so they could talk about boys and breakups. I didn't realize that blogging was the modern day equivalent of newspaper editorials or pamphlets like the one Thomas Paine wrote in the 1770s.

My first blog was called "From Where I Sit." It shared the same name as my weekly summary newsletter, and my goal was to transition the content I was sharing via email to my blog. The purpose of *From Where I Sit* was to share my opinion on things as I saw them from where I was in the world, i.e. from where I was sitting. I figured that if the writers on the major websites I was reading could do it, so could I, and I started publishing my own work.

It didn't take me long to realize I needed my own site. If I was going to create a place for my writing, I couldn't use a free subdomain for much longer. I'd never purchased a domain before, and I was pretty nervous. But, I moved forward and began writing anyway.

With each new post, I got stronger as a writer. I got better at communicating my thoughts and sharing what I was learning about leadership and personal development. Though my blog wouldn't gain much traction until much later in my journey, I still attracted a small number of readers. Mainly because I nagged them about reading my latest post, but that's what you have to do as a beginner.

I continued to write on and off through 2012 and 2013. I fumbled my way through things and didn't put much effort into learning the craft and improving my skills.

Whatever you're working on and whatever you're trying to accomplish, you can't stop learning. Regardless of how good you are, you can always improve. Professional athletes are always working on making tiny adjustments to their shots, swings, throws and every other aspect of the game. If you want to become a professional, act like one.

In May of 2013, I spent my first real money on improving my writing. Instead of another video game or a vacation, I enrolled in Jeff Goins' Tribe Writers course. To this day, I never finished it. Even still, what I learned in those first few weeks made a noticeable improvement in my writing. I learned to format my posts in a way that's easier to read. I gained the courage to write like I talk and share more of my personal stories.

Almost immediately after implemented the things I learned from Jeff, the number of people who visited my site tripled. I went from having just over 100 readers per month to over 300. Six months later, it tripled again. This increase in traffic and my ability to reach more people with my message was a direct result of an intense focus on improving my skills.

If you want to do better, become better. If you want to achieve more, learn more. As Maxwell wrote in The Law of the Lid in *The 21 Irrefutable Laws of Leadership,* we can only raise people up to the level we are, no higher. Maxwell wrote the Law about leadership, but it applies to our businesses as well. To build successful companies, lead teams, or even help people on their journey, we can only do so to the extent to which we've done it ourselves. Sometimes the best thing you can do to help other people is to help yourself. The more you know, the more you can teach.

While all of this was going on, a coworker of mine, Dave (not his real name), kept up with and followed my journey. He read my blog, he'd occasionally come to the book club meetings, and he was someone I could talk to about the books and blogs I read and the projects I was working on. Dave and I talked about leadership, both good and bad, and how we'd do things if we were in charge. Dave and I were friends.

I remember one particular training session Dave and I attended. We were going to learn about the new online ordering system and were to be updated on the way Dell was going to move forward. In the late 1990s, Dell was one of the largest e-commerce businesses in the world, and the execs wanted to boost automated selling efforts and reclaim that title.

Even now I place a heavy emphasis in automation. I like to show people how to do basic tasks so we can focus on things computers can't do for us, like solving problems and developing solutions. Dell's online ordering system was in perfect alignment with how I liked to do business. At one point, 89% of my sales revenue was coming from the online sources I set up for my clients. Now that's passive income!

But, during that training session, I realized just how differently Dave and I viewed business. I wanted to teach my clients to fish while he planned to carry the tackle box, bait the hook and even hold the pole for his clients if necessary.

My way allowed me to average 137% quota attainment for my tenure at Dell and pushed 89% of my orders via the online portal. I had the highest quota achievement of any salesperson on a team of over 150 and in a business unit that generated over $2 billion dollars in sales. I had an extremely high customer satisfaction rate, and I was always graded "very good" on my annual performance reviews. Teaching clients to fish was working, and it was working well.

After the training for the online ordering system, Dave and I agreed to disagree. He would continue holding his customers' hands and doing everything for them. He'd continue to get bogged down and overworked while I taught my clients how to help themselves so we could talk about solving larger problems. He was fine taking orders for $60 printer toner while I put in the advance work for my clients to be confident enough place a $1.2 million order for 1125 computers, online. But, to each his own.

So, I continued to blog and focus on personal growth. I wrote posts that were bold and unapologetic that would never get published out of fear of what the bosses would think. I wrote posts that were good but not great. And, I wrote posts that regurgitated information and ones that were uniquely my own. What I want to make clear is that I was a writer before I was a business owner. I was continuously creating new content and sharing information that helped other people.

In the fall of 2013, in November, I launched my podcast. After Ashley had bought me a microphone for my birthday, I knew I had to move forward. It was at this point in my online career that I either shit or got off the pot. I either did it, or I didn't. I either got serious about writing and helping people, or, I threw in the towel, sucked it up, and resigned myself to the fate of a Corporate drone for the next forty years.

But before I get ahead of myself, I must share how another nail was driven home to seal my fate.

Around the middle of 2013, my boss left the company. If you've worked for a corporation the size of Dell, you know this is the opportunity every promotion-eligible person looks for. In case you haven't, my boss leaving fell into the category of "death or retirement" which were two of the only ways someone in my position could get promoted. Needless to say, an open manager position created a vacuum that could only be filled by the networking and self-promotion frenzy of all senior sales people.

Though I was roughly ten years younger than Dave, I felt like we were on equal footing when applying for the job. He had additional experience, but I had recent success on my side.

After a long series of interviews, Dave got the job and became my manager. No big deal, right? We were friends, no hard feelings. In fact, congratulations! Now my friend was my manager, cool!

As with death and retirement, a promotion also creates a vacuum that must be filled. To fill that void, I took over Dave's now vacant territory and began working with the accounts he'd been handling for almost ten years.

Our difference in business strategy created a challenging transition for me. As I started to integrate my online strategies, I was met with some resistance. Customers who had been faxing in purchase orders for a decade were now somewhat skeptical about being able to order their items via the internet.

But, they came around. And, they came around fast. When given the opportunity to bring their ordering into the 21st century, they pounced on it. After Dell's fiscal quarter ended in July, I found myself as the most successful, highest attaining salesperson on my team. I over sold my quota by almost 70% and placed a single order for over $3.3 million.

Not only did I take over for Dave, but I replaced his way of doing business with my own. Though he and I didn't agree, I still crushed it where the quota was concerned. I had the best quarter of my career in the wake of losing out on promotion. With a $20,000 commission payout coming my way as 2013 came to a close, I was sitting on top of the world.

As I mentioned before, I launched my podcast in November. In December, at a hip restaurant with loud music in downtown Austin, I was awarded the "Team Rock Star" award for exceptional sales performance. Looking back at how things played out, it's funny that Dave was the one who chose me for the award. I guess it's hard to ignore the highest attaining salesperson on your team, even if you don't care for him. But we'll get to that.

In January, Ashley and I packed our bags and headed to Las Vegas for New Media Expo (NMX). Up until then, most of the connections I made online stayed online. But at NMX, all of that changed.

For the first time, I got to interact with people who were doing what I wanted to do; with entrepreneurs who were making an honest living online and doing what they loved.

New Media Expo 2014 was a magical time. As Ashley tells the story, I came out of my shell and was truly happy. I met readers of my blog and even a few listeners to my new podcast. In a rooftop bar, at a party overlooking Las Vegas sprawled below, I was recognized for the first time. It will be a long time before I forget that weekend and part of me hopes I'll always remember the magic it contained.

After a long weekend in Las Vegas, Ashley and I returned home, and I headed back to the office. When I got back to work, I no longer worked with the accounts I'd had so much success with six months before.

To drive another nail in my coffin, Dave moved me out of California and had me work with accounts in Arizona. Up until then, I had spent the last four years learning the California culture and had developed connections up and down the west coast. I knew the vendors, business contacts, third party resellers and I had a good reputation as someone who could get things done.

But that all meant nothing when I started working with accounts in Arizona. Not only was the culture different, the terrain unfamiliar and the geography one which I wasn't familiar with, but I was taking over a failing territory. The sales reps I was taking over for had reputations that were less than stellar and the customers had been leaving Dell for a competitor in droves. I was tasked with turning the ship around. Or so I was told.

Two weeks after returning from Las Vegas, I was fired. On Friday, January 17th at 9:12 a.m., as if I'd stolen trade secrets and sold them to the enemy, Dave escorted me out of the building.

Author's Note:

When first writing this chapter, I didn't realize how I had made things sound. Looking back, much of the last few pages makes it seem like I was a victim in all of this, and external events, outside my control, happened to me. My wife told me she thought I sounded bitter and a little angry.

Let me be clear. I did do something wrong. Was it fire-worthy? No, I don't think so. But I pushed the limits, and I got caught doing something I shouldn't have done.

However, I will admit to feeling bitter and angry. My pride and identity were closely tied to the company, even though I didn't enjoy working there. When Dave fired me, I was hurt, insulted, scared, and very bitter. And, it took me a long time to push past those feelings and move forward.

I added this Author's Note so I could be transparent with you. To show you it wasn't all roses and fun times after I left.

To paraphrase a Chinese proverb, a wise man looks not where he fell, but where he stumbled. In January of 2014, I stumbled. Hard. But with great friends, an incredible mastermind, and a supportive wife, I worked through it.

What I've now come to realize is that it's often our areas of greatest pain and embarrassment that are the same areas from where we can draw incredible strength. Our stories of heartache and struggle are the same stories which will allow us to connect with others in a very real way.

Don't hide your story. Don't hold back your pain. There is someone out there who needs to hear what you're going through.

12: BLINDSIDED

Never look back unless you are planning to go that way.
- Henry David Thoreau

One of the strategies I used while at Dell to become so successful was that I was always learning. Not only was I passionate about the technology and the products we sold, but I was doing extracurricular activities that improved my skills.

In addition to the book club and blogging, I was reading voraciously. I attended an EntreLeadership One-Day event hosted by Dave Ramsey and his team, and, through my podcast, I was learning from experts and millionaires all over the world. These types of activities helped me stay head and shoulders above my peers and stand out from the crowd. I could never pinpoint the resources that helped me because there were always so many.

However, what I can pinpoint is the one resource that became the final blow that sealed my fate.

A few months prior, Jeff Goins hosted a training call about how to increase book sales by sending out free trials. I logged in over my lunch hour and semi-listened while I worked. I don't remember much about the call, but I distinctly remember what happened afterward.

When Ashley and I returned from New Media Expo, and I went back to work, I began to notice things weren't quite right. On Thursday, January 9th, one of the days when we could work from home instead of commuting to the office, I got a call from Dave. He said he wasn't seeing the results he'd hoped for when he moved from me from familiar California to unknown Arizona. Dave said he wanted to sit down with me and figure out a plan for improvement and ended the call.

The following Tuesday I got another call from Dave. He said,

"I was listening to your calls from previous months and hoping to find something we could help train you on, and I found something. Feel free to stop me if you know what it is."

In the moments that followed, I distinctly heard the playback of Jeff Goins' voice as he welcomed everyone to the call I'd dialed into months before. Jeff thanked us for joining him and laid out what we'd learn by tuning in.

Dave asked me what the call was about and why I joined. I explained that the call was about generating sales by sending out "seeds," or free trial equipment, to prospects hoping they would eventually buy. I stretched the truth a little, but I didn't lie and said that such practices were standard in how Dell was gaining new customers and selling new lines of business.

And that's true. During my time in sales at the company, my team and I had "seeded" hundreds of thousands of dollars' worth of equipment to hundreds of customers in an effort to win new business.

While only loosely related to work, Jeff's call was related to what I was doing in my job. But there was a problem, and it was twofold. Problem one - my boss, Dave, knew I was a writer. Problem two - I had dialed in while on a company phone. Had either one of those problems not been present, my future would have been drastically different.

Two days after that fateful conversation, Dave called me on the phone again and requested a face to face meeting first thing the next morning. Over the next several hours my stomach churned, and the writing on the wall became clearer than ever. Ashley and I talked, shed tears and feared for our future.

On Friday, I showed up early. On the off-chance I was wrong, and I wasn't getting canned, I wanted to be punctual. Ya, that doesn't make sense to me either.

At 9:02 am, Dave called me into a small conference room just off of the main sales floor. Few people from my team were in the office that early so there weren't many people to see me take my final walk. Dave opened the conference room door, and there sat the same human resources person who I'd met before and who, unbeknownst to me, was also on the phone when Dave replayed Jeff Goins' recorded voice.

There was no back and forth and no discussion. I pleaded my case, but their minds were set. Despite the history we'd shared as friends and coworkers, Dave dismissed me with finality. My desk would be packed up and shipped to my house, and he would tell my teammates his version of how everything had played out during the morning meeting.

As of 9:12, I was unemployed.

As of 9:13, I was in my car and headed home to my new job as owner and employee of the soon-to-be-formed DwizzyWid Media, LLC.

I was unemployed for about sixty seconds, and how I made the transition is what this book is about.

By now you may be wondering why I shared my story with you. If you aren't, you should. If you're going to succeed in business and life, you have to start prioritizing your time immediately. And, now that you've spent the last few hours reading about my journey, there needs to be a reason.

I shared my story because I want to make it clear that I'm just like you. I went to school, earned a degree, got a job and did what I was told. I excelled at my work and, for the most part, did what I loved. I made one mistake, and it cost me everything. Or, so I thought. I shared my story because I want you to see that I was average. I wasn't special, and I had no unique skills. I want you to know that anything I've done, and anything I've accomplished, you can do and accomplish too.

Now the fun begins. Now the rubber meets the road, and it's time to get to work.

Are you with me? Let's do this.

PART II - LET'S GET TO WORK

Be miserable. Or motivate yourself. Whatever has to be done, it's always your choice.
- Wayne Dyer

Before we move on, let me share with you a story that has stuck with me over the past several years. Anytime I meet someone who feels as if they're going nowhere in life, or that they've become comfortable in their discomfort this story helps put things into perspective.

The Dog and the Nail

Once upon a time, two old men were sitting out on the front porch and looking at the sunset. As the two men rocked in their chairs, the first man's dog, who was laying on the wooden boards that made the porch, started to whimper.

After sitting in the breeze listening to the dog whimper for several minutes, the second man turned to the first and asked, "What's wrong with your dog?"

"He's lying on a nail" the first man replied.

"Is he crippled?"

"Nope."

With a look of confusion on his face, the second man continued. "Then, why doesn't he just move?"

"Well, because he's just not that miserable yet."

***

I remember when I first heard that story; it was like a much-needed punch to the gut. How many times in your life have you been stuck, just sitting there in your misery, but unwilling to do anything about it?

Hey, I'm not placing any blame or pointing any fingers (unless you're one of my coaching clients). I was that dog on the nail for two years at Dell before getting fired.

I had enough energy to piss and moan, but not ever enough desire to do anything to improve my situation. For two years leading up to my "exit," I talked about looking for jobs outside of Dell. Ashley and I had many conversations about making a change, and yet I did nothing.

I was just like the dog on the porch laying on the nail. I knew I could do my job in my sleep and do it well enough to make a decent salary without much effort. I knew if I switched jobs I might make more money, but I'd have to learn a new corporate system, learn new tools and resources, and, in the end, I wouldn't be any closer to turning my blog into a business. I wasn't happy where I was, but I wasn't miserable enough to do anything productive about it.

So, I stayed on my nail.

The legendary sales coach, Jim Rohn, once said, "You are not a tree! Get up and move!" Too many people, including myself, forget that we have the ability to change our situation in life if we're willing to do something about it. The crazy part is, we're each where we are because of what we've done, and it's our fault!

One of my old bosses used to say, "The doors don't lock from the outside," meaning we were free to leave at any time. While that wasn't the most motivating thing he could say, it's the truth. We weren't prisoners there, and by staying, we were, in a way, condoning every bit of misery that came our way.

As you begin mapping out this next leg of your exit strategy, keep the story of the dog and the nail in your mind. Are you motivated enough to putt things in place and take the actions necessary for you to live the life you were meant to live?

I hope you are! Let's get started.

13: THE ONLY BUSINESS MODEL THAT WORKS

Get better at the basics and teach them. If you're not going to teach someone for free, someone else will
- John Lee Dumas

I'm often asked about the key to success. From accomplished hosts on podcasts to casual conversation, people of all ages and from across a variety of industries have asked me about the secret sauce that will make them successful in business so they can do what they love.

I only took one semester of business school. I made it halfway through and realized most of what I'd learned was not to lie, cheat or steal and don't do business with people who do. But after being in sales for almost twenty years, and owning my own business for the past several, I have learned that people do business with people who are like them. Business is done human to human.

When I get asked about the secret sauce, my "key to success,", and I tell people what I'm about to share with you, they rarely want to hear it. They're often in search of the quick fix, the fast cash, and the instant success that doesn't exist anywhere but in their heads.

I can't blame them, though; I wanted it too. But, we have to accept that the road is tough and move forward.

The key to success is to put in the time and effort and hard work up font, to provide tremendous value first, and follow the freemium model of business.Today, the only business model that works is the "freemium" model.

This odd-sounding word is taking the online world by storm and is the way hundreds of online entrepreneurs are building successful, growing and thriving businesses.

The freemium model is a pricing strategy where a company offers some or part of their products or services for free, but the premium content has a cost associated with it.

For example, online business mogul and expert on creating passive income, Pat Flynn was blogging and providing resources, tools, and helpful reviews years before he had a product he could charge people for. And, when he did, he had built up so much personal brand equity that he was able to sell his ebook and make over $8000 the first month after launching his product.

Another example is former CEO of Thomas Nelson Publishing Company, Michael Hyatt. Long before Michael released a product, he added value wherever he could online and in the real world. He blogged about topics such as leadership and self-publishing. He connected with fellow bloggers and writers and helped them improve their craft. After building an audience of people who knew, liked and trusted him, Michael was able to grow a multi-million dollar business around his brand.

In the traditional sense, the freemium way of doing business has been around for decades, though we didn't call it that.

Brick and mortar stores have used the freemium model since the first craftsman decided to give a free sample of his product. If you've ever been to a Sam's Club or Costco on a weekend, you've probably been enticed with samples of all kinds. Give someone a free taste, whet their appetite and offer them the rest of the meal at a premium.

Hollywood has been using the freemium model since the first movie preview was released to the public. Hook people with the promise of an incredible on-screen adventure, give them a free sneak preview of what's to come and then charge them to get the full experience.

Movie producers have also used the freemium model for years. When Sylvester Stallone wanted to make the first *Rocky* movie he had to sell a studio on the idea for free before he sold them the script for money. He had to paint a mental picture for the studio heads and give enough of the story for the decision makers to see his vision for the movie.

Before we buy a new television, we want to see it. Before we buy a new book, we read the first few pages. Before we purchase a car, we test-drive it.

Stallone had worked for free before he made it big. Hyatt had written for free before he made it big. Flynn had researched, tested and shared before he made it big.

When you're starting out, you too will have to work for free before you make it big. Your business model works only if it's based on the freemium model. People will only know, like and trust you if they can clearly see who you are and what you're about. No secrets, no deception.

Particularly in a business where your goal is to get paid for what you know, your ideas are your product and your words are your content. Instead of making computers or baking cookies to show what you can do, you must write and record.

In today's modern world, one in which "spam" hardly means a canned meat anymore, you have to embrace a new way of doing business. The old concepts of bait and switch no longer work. Scammy and slimy salespeople no longer win. When information is everywhere, the seller is no longer in control, the buyer is. Openness and transparency are the ways you will build your business.

Give your best and give it freely. Show your audience that a relatively unknown person and business are worth paying attention to. Be human. We want to do business with other human beings and so do your customers.

14: THE BEST WAY TO GET STARTED

*People need stories more than bread itself. They tell us
how to live, and why.*
- Arabian Nights

S ince the first person scratched the surface of one rock with another, humans have been writing. Words, symbols, and pictures have been the tools we've used to communicate with one another for centuries.

Now, we have the internet, and surprisingly little has changed. Words are still the best way to express an idea and reach an audience. Specifically, the written word is the best form of communication we have here in the first half of the 21st century.

Even with the popularity of video, and the increasing popularity of streaming video, text still dominates. Though printed material may be going out of style, ebooks are flying off digital shelves at a steady rate.

For this reason, the best way for you to get started, the best way for you to start building your brand, your business, and influence, is through the power of words. And, the best platform for you to use is a blog.

you must blog

Why Blogging?

Creating video content takes three things: a person behind the camera, a person or subject in front of the camera, and the camera. You may be able to get by with only two of those things with a little ingenuity, but you'll still need talent and technical know-how.

While most cell phones have cameras on them, you've still got to edit the video and have a place to host it. The barrier to getting started with video isn't too high, but the barrier is still there.

Creating picture content takes the same three things. You have to have a camera and a subject, but you also need to have picture taking talent. Yes, anyone can tap the capture button on a phone or click the shutter release on a DSLR, but not everyone can take a picture that will build a platform.

Because anyone and everyone can take photos and upload them to a free photo sharing site or social network, it's harder to stand out. It doesn't take much time, effort or talent to snap a picture or upload a "selfie," so everyone does. It doesn't take much skill to start, but it takes a lot of talent to stand out.

While that last part rings true for anything, the easiest way for you to get started with an online business is with a blog.

Here's why: Anyone with an internet connection can start a blog.

That's it! You can't have an internet connection without a device, and just about any device can be used to get started.

Now, don't get me wrong, blogging can be difficult, but so can anything else. Anything worth doing is going to be a challenge. The best things in life are the things we have to work for, and building your business is no exception.

Seriously, Why Blogging?

A blog is essentially words on a web page. Since search engines can't hear, your podcast can't drive your SEO (search engine optimization) efforts. Since search engines can't see, your videos won't be able to help you. Yes, you should be doing both of these things; audio and video should be on your list of things to do, but they shouldn't be where you start.

Before we move forward, let's talk about YouTube and the differences between text, audio and video.

YouTube is one of the top five most popular websites in the world.[3] It is also said to be the second most popular search engine in the world with over 1 billion visitors per month. YouTube also reaches more viewers than any other cable network in the United States, and they cover 95% of the internet-using population.[4] Online video is a beast.

But, again, I'm not saying you shouldn't be using video. What I'm advocating is that you don't use video alone to build your business. Unless you already have video equipment and have a talent for video, my suggestion is to use video to enhance your other efforts. Even with the power and popularity of YouTube, the text still drives results. Titles, tags, links and summary bios drive traffic to videos, not the moving pictures themselves.

Text on a page, like you're reading here or as you would read on a blog post, can be measured in bytes and kilobytes (1000 bytes). Text pages are made up of a finite number of simple symbols that can be broken down into ones and zeros.

Images are measured in kilobytes and megabytes (1 million bytes); video in megabytes and even gigabytes (1 billion bytes). Even if a search engine could understand images, and they're

---

[3] www.alexa.com/siteinfo/youtube.com#trafficstats

[4] www.youtube.com/yt/press/statistics.html

starting to, they could read one million pages of text in the time it takes to read one image that is one megabyte in size. If one blog post is comparable to a single page to read, analyze and catalog (called indexing), a picture is like a million pages, and a video is potentially billions.

Not only is it literally impossible (with current technology) to completely index an image or a video, but it's a practical impossibility. Especially since, according to video marketing firm ReelSEO, over 300 hours' worth of video is uploaded to YouTube every minute.[5] The only way YouTube can connect your video with the people who want to see it is through text headlines, text descriptions, and text tags.

Should you keep video in the back of your mind? Absolutely.

Should you start with video? No.

Blogging allows you to share a message via a medium that is universally recognizable by both humans and computers. Blogging gives you the ability to communicate, instruct, teach and motivate in a way that no other online media can with the technology available today.

By blogging, you can build a following, establish yourself as an authority in whatever niche you choose, and lay the groundwork for your business.

Here's the bottom line…

Any reputable business is expensive to build. It'll either cost your time, money, or both. There are no shortcuts.

What I'm advocating here is that you spend a little of both instead of a lot of either. By reading this book, I'm saving you hours (if not months or years) of time, and hopefully hundreds (if not thousands or hundreds of thousands) of dollars.

Instead of suggesting you spend $50,000 and go back to school, or take out a $100,000 loan for retail space, I'm showing you how

---

[5] Find more information at http://www.reelseo.com/youtube-300-hours/

to start your business for less than $500. Instead of taking on debt and holding a warehouse full of inventory that's declining in value with every passing hour, I want you to build a business with little to no overhead and no inventory to monitor or maintain.

No Products.

< 500⁰⁰

Why You Should Be Blogging

Blogging allows you to build an audience around the world with little to no startup costs. You can reach a global audience without ever having to leave the comfort of the couch.

People across the country can discover you and start following you. Readers in other countries can translate your words into their language with software built right into their web browser.

Your blog can be your home base - the place you send people who are interested in what you're doing and sharing on social media.

A blog can showcase your work. You can upload images of the paintings your working on, the sculptures you're sculpting, and the movies you're recording.

Your blog is your website; it's a digital storefront and a place online you control and can call your own. Instead of worrying about what changes Facebook or Twitter are going to make to your newsfeed, you can focus on the place you control. Your site is yours; you're in the driver's seat.

Yes, all of this is possible, and I'm living proof. Before I started my blog in 2012, I'd never bought a domain, never heard of hosting, and I wasn't on Twitter. The only other times I'd talked to someone outside of the United States was when I was on vacation out of the country and when I was in elementary school and had a Czechoslovakian pen pal.

Because of my blog, I have close friends around the country, good friends around the world, and an audience in over 190 countries. Without my blogs, I'd be bouncing from one job to another, not realizing the world of possibilities were hidden just on the other side of taking a chance.

Everything I've done, you can do too. And it all starts with a blog.

15: THINKING LIKE A CREATOR (AND WHAT TO CREATE)

Talent is cheaper than table salt. What separates the talented individual from the successful one is a lot of hard work.
- Stephen King

You stare at the blank page, and it stares right back, unintimidated. Your fingers hover over the keyboard, and you nervously await the wave of fantastic ideas you're sure is just over the horizon.

Many of the people who come to me for help with their content creation efforts struggle with what to create. They don't know where to start. These aspiring writers, podcasters, YouTubers, attorneys, chiropractors, etc., have all stalled for one of two reasons. They either have too many ideas or too few.

If you fall into one of those categories, or somewhere in between, relax. Many a great writer has stared at the blank page, waiting for a visit from their muse.

But waiting for your "muse" is like a professional athlete waiting until she "feels like it" before going to the gym or showing up for practice. If you want to be a serious writer, you have to get serious about writing. If your goal is to become a serious entrepreneur, you have to get serious about business building. You can't just show up when the weather is good or when your mood is right. You have to show up every day.

To help you with your writing (or other content creation efforts), I'm going to share some things to help you get going and which will help you build momentum. If blogging isn't how you plan on creating content, just swap the word "posts" below for "videos," audio recordings," or whatever else fits your business.

We'll cover:

- Popular types of posts (videos, episodes, images, etc.) that attract clients

- Templates and outlines you can use that provide structure to your content

- The one thing every piece of content your produce should have

- Topics you should write or record about

- Tools and resources that will help you build authority

After this chapter, you should know not only what to write about, but how to craft your posts into communication tools that will help you build your brand and help you establish yourself as an authority to whom people should pay attention.

Content Types

Writing posts and creating new content can get stale after a while if you don't mix things up with different kinds of posts. Remember, this is your blog and your business, so you are only limited by your own creativity.

Here are some different post types to help you keep things new, fresh, diverse and useful to your audience. Again, you should substitute the word "posts" for the kind of content that is the best fit for your message.

Lists

Create a list of books, tools, websites, resources, movies, etc. your ideal client, your "avatar," should check out or ones that have impacted you in a positive way. The "Types of" type of list post can help your clients discover new things. For example, "10 Types of Financial Tools You Can Use to…" List posts are an excellent way to show what you know while providing a shortcut for your readers. They should be easy to scan, and they also make great YouTube videos and infographics.

How Tos

Over half of the millennial generation believes they can find whatever they need on YouTube. How to posts are perfect for showcasing your expertise through demonstration. You can use a single video or a series of them, images, or simple text instructions.

FAQ/SAQs

Frequently asked and should ask questions are popular posts because they not only provide answers but also give the reader questions they didn't even know they needed to ask. For example, if you wrote a post called "14 Questions You Should Ask Before Buying Your First Car," you help new car buyers and establish yourself as an authority in the automotive industry. FAQ and SAQ posts allow you to direct the conversation the way you want it to go.

Checklists

Similar to the list post, the checklist post is more for listing items required for a particular action. For example, before our first camping trip as a couple, my wife and I printed off a checklist of must-have camping gear and went to the store. The checklist saved us time and helped us prepare. Your checklist should do the same thing.

Multi-Part Series

People love trilogies, quadrilogies, anthologies and multi-part series. These series also work for blog posts because they keep the reader coming back for more, plus they keep people on your site longer with a web of interconnected links.

Fix-It Posts

I learned how to drain a hot water heater by watching a fix-it video on YouTube. These types of posts don't have to be videos, so don't worry. Show your reader how to fix a problem they're having, and you're instantly a hero.

Top 10s

Similar to the list and checklist posts, Top 10 posts are a list of resources, but only the best. Top 10 posts are lists of items collected and curated by you. People love reading Top 10s because they know they're about to get the best resources, not the crappy ones, and they know the list won't take them a long time to get through. Since ten is a definite number, people figure the post is a quick read. Plus, these are opinion posts, and everyone likes to share what they think.

Quote Responses

Everybody loves a good quote. Quotes inspire and motivate people all the time. Share a quote you love, or one that's helped you in some way, write your response and explain what it means to you. Or, share a quote with which you disagree and tell the world why you think it's wrong. Don't be afraid of polarizing your audience; strong opinions create engagement and lead to raving fans.

Test/Results Posts

I love a good test/results post. Anytime I get the opportunity to see the results from an expert, I jump on it. Experimentation also helps you build authenticity alongside your authority. When people know you're not perfect, they're more likely to relate to you.

Personal Stories

The people reading your blog are there for information, correct, but they're also there because they like you and are interested in what you're doing. When Ashley and I were in Costa Rica, I shared a post of the two of us standing atop a beautiful waterfall, and my audience loved it! You can be an expert and still be human, so write a personal post to share about your life.

Recaps

Almost every article on a news site is a recap of recent events. You can do the same thing after a conference or workshop you attend. Share the highlights, the benefits of attending, and make a recommendation as to whether you'd go again next time.

Product Reviews

If you plan on making any money with affiliate marketing, the product review post is a must. Even if affiliate commissions aren't on your radar, or if they don't fit with your business, they're still a good way to show your reader the best option among many. Share your favorite product alongside its competitors and why you like it. Anyone who reads your post will see you as a trusted source they can go to when they need help making a decision.

While these are some of my favorite types of posts, there are all sorts of ways you can create content that helps you connect with your audience and market your products. For more content ideas check out my post *129 Blog Post Ideas to Help You Get Started,*[6] and *The Ultimate List of Blog Post Ideas* on digitalmarketer.com.[7]

Templates

Templates allow you to automate, scale, and produce consistent results over time. Even when you're in the beginning stages of your business, you need to develop a system that will allow you to provide a quality product on a consistent and regular basis.

Think of a template as your recipe. The way a master chef can create the same delicious dessert each and every time is through the use of a recipe. Sure, there can be a tiny bit of room for artistry and innovation, but the results remain outstanding time and time again.

Templates also enable you to work with speed and efficiency. They remove the guesswork and provide a structure that has been proven to provide excellent results. Like a chef has different recipes

---

[6] https://www.ellorywells.com/129-blog-post-ideas/
[7] https://www.digitalmarketer.com/blog-post-ideas/

for different dishes, your template can change depending on the type of post you're writing.

Most post types will follow a typical structure of opening, image, story, content, close, and question. You can play around with it, but that configuration is proven to draw readers in, inform them, and then engage them. If you'd like to download the Evernote template I use to outline and write my posts, you can find it at www.theexitstrategybook.com/appendix-b.

My last piece of advice regarding templates is to create one for every task you do more than once. Instead of asking yourself, "how do I do this?" or "how did I do this last time?" you can pull up your template so you can do it the same way again and again. Your customers want consistency from you, and a template is the best way for you to give it to them.

The One Thing (CTA)

Every post you write should have a call to action (CTA). If you write a post without asking your reader to do something, you've just wasted an opportunity to connect with them again further down the road.

The goal with your blog shouldn't be to get new readers. Your goal should be to get new readers who keep coming back for more, time and time again.

This goal also applies to the emails you send to your list. Having a call to action with everything you create is a good business strategy. If you don't know what type of CTA to include, start simple with an "If you liked this, then you'll LOVE this [insert link]."

Give your readers something to do, a way to stay connected, or another resource to check out, and they're more likely to do it than if you leave them to figure it out on their own.

Topics

We've already talked about creating content that sells, but what else should you write or record about? Your readers don't want to read about who you are, what you do or where you came from every single day. So, what else should fill up your blog?

After you've invested the time to figure out who your avatar is, you should have a pretty good idea about what they need. Once you know what they need, you can create resources to meet those needs. If your audience needs help figuring out the best email marketing service for their small business, you could create a list post that outlines the various options. You could go a step further and write a Top 10 or Product Review post and include an affiliate link to your recommended solution.

If your avatar needs to know what kind of stretches they can do from their cubicle to reduce back pain, write a Fix-It or How To post with "The Top 3 Exercises Everyone Can Do From Almost Anywhere." The possibilities are endless when you begin to think outside the box.

Another way to come up with topics is to think about all of the problems you've had regarding your niche. Come up with a list and share your experiences surrounding each item on your list. The odds are if you had a problem or challenge, your audience has too. Every problem you solve for yourself is a problem you can solve for someone else.

Authority-Building Tools

Blogging and creating online content aren't like the research projects you may remember from school. There aren't usually any citations and peer-reviewed articles aren't required.

However, not everything we learned about writing in school needs to be unlearned. There is a lot to be said about citing references and linking to credible sites to boost your own authority. If you're going to build your business around a blog, here are some things you should use.

Outbound links

Linking from your posts to other sites will not only help with your SEO, but it will help your authority. Anyone can write their opinion and hit publish, but only experts will take the time to support their views with documented fact. Even when you are writing your opinion, linking to someone else's blog where they share a similar view will help you out.

Inbound links

Anytime you link to a relevant post or page on your own site you're boosting your authority. If you've written on a topic more than once, you can show your expertise. Plus, by linking within your site, you're able to keep people on your site for longer, which reduces bounce rate, increases page views, and several other things that help with your domain's authority on the web.

Passive language   No Passive language!

Whenever you sit down to write or record, consider the words you use and eliminate any passive language in your writing. Don't use phrases like "I think…" or "In my opinion…" Those words are unnecessary, they'll hurt your credibility and will hinder your efforts to build authority. Instead of "I think the best web hosting company is…" say, "The best hosting company is…" and reinforce your statement with examples and facts. Eliminate the word "just" from your vocabulary. Rarely say "that" as it's usually incorrect to include it. Use the Hemingway App[8] to help you find and eliminate adverbs as well, as they seldom make your writing more compelling.

Tell a story to draw your readers in, and then once you've got their attention, hit them with the lesson to be learned. Be useful, be helpful, but above all else, be yourself.

Blog Post Template

Opening
Image
Story
Content
Close
question.

---

[8] Use the Hemingway App for free in your browser or purchase it for offline use at http://www.hemingwayapp.com/

16: BECOMING A STORYTELLER

The more I told my story, the stronger I got. Every time I tell my story, I learn something new about myself.
- Mylee "YC" Cardenas

People want to be entertained before they want to be informed. That's why the sales of a best-selling documentary pale in comparison to even a low budget action movie. Audiences want a hero to root for, an insurmountable obstacle keeping the underdog down, a complicated situation without a way out, or impending doom that must be stopped. What I've just outlined is the basis of any successful movie. These concepts are archetypes the human psyche loves. If you can create a compelling story every time you write a post, record a podcast, or shoot a video, you'll have an audience who relates to you and who keeps coming back for more.

Now that you know the strategies behind creating content and getting more traffic let's look at what matters more than almost everything else - the story.

It doesn't matter how much traffic you're getting if you visitors never return a second time. The key to building a business or a profitable website is repeated business - people coming back over and over again. If you aren't telling a story that draws people in, and you aren't telling stories that sell, you'll fail. Don't worry, a good story can be as simple as how you source your produce from local farmers. Or, your story could be as complex as traveling the world to take pictures of the most exotic wildlife. Either way, here's how to prevent failure and queue your business up for success.

The 5 Ws

The key to content that tells a story and sells can be found all the way back in our elementary school days. While most people may only remember nouns, verbs, adjectives or maybe how to diagram a sentence, the writers among us will remember something different. When you're just starting and looking for topics to cover, remember the Five Ws and the H. What are they? I'm sure you can guess, but let's take a look.

The five Ws are who, what, when, where and why. The H is how. These six elements will help you craft a story that connects with a global audience, attracts visitors, and converts subscribers into clients. By using these six elements, you can build a business.

Who

Your audience wants to know who you are, and they want to know about your experiences. They want to know what you stand for and what you're all about. They want to know what makes you tick, what you enjoy and what you like to do. If the same thing that makes you tick makes them tick, and they like the same stuff, you're alike! And, being alike makes us like you.

They also want to know who your clients are. Your audience and prospective customers want to know if the problems they're facing are ones you've dealt with before and handled successfully.

They want to know that if they come to you with their problems, you'll be able to help. Your audience wants to like you, and when they learn who you are, they will start to.

What

Your audience wants to know what you do. Your future clients want to know what makes you an expert. They're curious to know the results you've gotten for yourself and for other people. They want to read testimonials and hear your clients talk about the results you've helped them achieve. Because, if you helped them get great results, you can help us get great results too.

Your audience is interested in knowing what you know and how you learned it. They want to know the experiences that shaped you into the expert you are today. They need to believe in you, and when they see what you know and what you can do to help people, they will start to.

When

Your readers, listeners, and prospective clients want to know when you started. If you just started, it will be harder for them to trust you. But, if you've been in the game for forever, we'll wonder if you're current and relevant. I know, it's a fine line.

They want to know you're experienced and knowledgeable and not still wet behind the ears. They want to know you've "been there, done that, and have the t-shirt." Your audience wants to know when you got started because dates put things in perspective. When they know you've seen success that gives them both a challenge and confirmation. They'll think, "If you did it in two, maybe I can hustle and do it in one." Plus, if you got to where you are in just in just a few years, it proves that it's possible and that they can do it too.

Your audience wants to trust you, and when they learn that you've got some experience under your belt, even if it's just a little bit, they will start to.

Where

Your readers will always be curious to know where you learned how to do what you do. If you both went to the same school, you have something in common, and maybe you can be buddies! If you both follow the same people and read the same books, they'll believe you can be friends!

By the way, it's ok to be friends with the people in your community. In fact, I encourage it. Some of my best friends are readers of my blog, and some of my readers have become great friends.

The members of your community want to know where in the world you live. If you're both in the south, you're automatically alike and have something in common. If you're both in the east, you can laugh about those westerners. If you came from the same town or even the same state, you're basically best friends. Finding common ground is the first step in building relationships.

They are also interested in learning where you are on your journey. If you're just starting out, so are they and maybe you can grow together? If you're a few steps ahead, you can teach me what you know. If you've built what they want to build, then they know they can do it too.

Your readers, listeners, clients and community members want to know, like and trust you. And when they learn where you've come from and where you're going, they'll start to.

Why

Why are you so passionate about what you do? Why do you care so much? Your audience wants to know what events in your life are driving you to make changes and succeed. They want to know why you give a damn.

If you've been through tough times, so have they, and that means you're alike. They want to know that not everything has been roses and honey for you. They want to know you've had your share of thorns and stings, too. If they think your life has been perfect, you audience won't be able to relate to you because their lives haven't been.

They want to know why people need you. They're curious about what draws other people toward you. If what attracted existing readers and clients to you is the same thing that drives your prospective readers, then maybe they can be friends and form a community. Connecting the members of your community to one another is how you build raving fans and grow your business. Plus, if what drew them in also draws in new community members, then they know they're not alone in what they're working on. When one relationship leads to another, a tribe is born!

How

Your customers, clients, readers, and friends really want to know how you got to where you are. They want to know the tools you used so they can use them too. They want to know the books you've read and the people you've connected with so they can read and connect with them too. And they're curious about how you do it. If you're successful, and you tell them the tools you use, then they'll want to use those tools too. And, if they use the same tools the successful person uses, then they can be successful too.

They want to know the steps you took so they can take them. Your readers want to know the path you took so they can follow it too.

They also want to know how you can help them. They want to know if they come to you with a problem, you can guide them to a solution.

They want to know how you do what you do you, and when they hear about the tools you use, they'll want to start using them too.

***

We all love a good story, and when it comes to starting your own business, online or otherwise, you need to share your story. Whether it's because people want to root for an underdog, or they like a peek behind the curtain, people love stories. Your readers want a good story before they want to read the lesson behind it. If you can share your journey, including the ups and downs, you'll connect better with your audience and be more memorable.

Think back to when you were last in school. Picture your most memorable teacher. I bet the person you're thinking of stands out in your mind because they either were funny or they could always tell a good story that kept you on the edge of your seat. If you want a captive audience, share a story. If your desire is to connect with your audience, share *your* story.

And, as with any great story, yours must have heroes, villains, risk, reward, and plenty of suspense. When you share your story, you separate yourself from the "also-rans", the other bloggers who want to sit on their high-horse without connecting with their audience.

When you share your journey, you're no longer just another blogger or podcaster. Your story creates an opportunity for your audience to transition from knowing what you do to liking who you are and then trusting how you will help them.

If you can bring your audience along for the ride, and if you can let them share in your highs and lows, successes and failures, they'll be your fans for life. I know because my fans tell me.

Jack Daniels and Tabasco Sauce

I'm not much of a fan of hard liquor; my throat and stomach just can't take it. And, I prefer salsa to spicy sauces. Because of those two preferences, I've never had much desire to drink Jack Daniels or eat anything with Tabasco sauce on it. I'm more of a beer, wine, and mixed drink kind of guy than a Jack and Coke drinker.

Though I don't care for either of those products, I do care about the lesson in story telling I got while visiting Avery Island, Louisiana while in my twenties.

My mom, grandma, and I had driven to Louisiana to take my sister to summer camp, and on the way back to Texas we decided to stop at the McIlhenny Company factory to see how they made their world-famous Tabasco. We were able to walk through parts of the plant and see some of the factory floor. We saw all types of Tabasco sauce and got to see how it was made, stored, bottled and served. We even got to try Tabasco ice cream at their tiny shop on the hill. Yes, it was disgusting.

Our tour guide told us that after the peppers are picked and processed, the precursor to Tabasco sauce is stored in the oak barrels they get from the Jack Daniels factory in Tennessee. Instead of throwing them away or disassembling them, Jack Daniels ships the barrels down to Louisiana to hold the Tabasco sauce as it cures while sealed under two inches of salt.

I don't know how many years it's been since we took that weekend trip, but I still remember it. And, even though I don't drink Jack or eat Tabasco, I tell that story to anyone I'm with who I see eating or drinking them.

With their factory tour, Tabasco was able to make a fan out of me even though I don't use their sauce. Because I got to see how the proverbial sausage was made, I felt like I was a tiny part of their story. I knew things about Tabasco other people didn't know, and that made me feel cool. And, because I've seen the process and quality of Tabasco, if I were ever to start using a hot sauce instead of salsa, there's really only one product I'd consider.

The tour of Avery Island and the McIlhenny Tabasco plant showed me all of the elements of a great story. Every year, thousands of visitors get to see who the founders were and why they started making Tabasco. We learned about the process and where the peppers came from. We got to see how the peppers are chosen, how they're prepared, and how they're cured to become the world-famous product.

When you can draw people in and show them the human side of your business, and when you can illustrate how you do what you do and why you're doing it, you will create content that sells. Plus, you'll be one step closer to creating fans for life.

PART III - THE ROADMAP

Give me six hours to chop down a tree and I will spend
the first four sharpening the ax.
*- **Abraham Lincoln***

From the very beginning, I've wanted *Exit Strategy* to help as many people as possible. No more sick-to-your-stomach feelings when you log into your work computer. No more dreaded meetings that accomplish nothing. And no more bosses who treat you like crap. Well, as I sat down and reviewed the outline for the book and how it would be laid out, I couldn't help but notice a glaring error. An error that I've corrected with the addition of Part III - The Roadmap.

In this section of the book, we're going to map out the timeline I wish I'd followed from the very beginning. I'll share what to do, when you should to it, the tools you should use, and how you can move forward along a timeline to help you turn your exit strategy plans into an exit strategy reality. You'll get my recommendations for every step along the way.

My Roadmap includes blogging. It's how I got started, it's what led to me signing my first client, and blogging is how I'd do it if I had to do it all over again.

If you're not a writer, anytime I refer to blogging, imagine I'm referring to video or audio content. My intent is not to make a writer out of you if you don't want to be one. My goal is to show you how you can use various types of content to establish your authority, help you share your expertise and your message, and build a following of loyal supporters, clients, and friends.

While I may say blogging, don't get caught up on the word itself. Instead, I encourage you to apply the principles to whatever form of content you choose to create.

Each chapter in Part III is meant to be an outline and a task list for a single week. You can move things around and shift your schedule, but what I've attempted to do here is give you a roadmap for how to proceed. I have done my best to put things into an order that will allow you to get the maximum impact and results for your time. There is no magic bullet and no secret formula that will get the job done, but this Roadmap is how I'd do it if forced to do it all over again from day one.

Whether you decide to take it slow and spread everything out over the next several weeks, or you choose to burn the midnight oil and cram it all in as fast as possible, here is an outline of what your future holds:

- **Week 1:** You'll lay the groundwork for your business. You'll do a couple of things that may be confusing and that you won't use for awhile, but you'll be glad you did them when the time comes. Mysterious, right?

- **Week 2:** You'll begin to outline and schedule your content over the next several weeks. You'll nail down your avatar and determine how you can best serve them. And, you'll put the pieces together so you can begin building your email list.

- **Week 3:** I'll share with you some of the "must-use" plugins for WordPress. You'll start the writing, recording, building, etc., that make up the majority of your content creation efforts. Week 3 is also the week when you'll get your logo.

- **Week 4:** This week is all about creating the content that will serve as your samples. These taste tests will showcase your skills and talents.

- **Week 5:** After you've been locked away in your workspace for four weeks, you'll go outside and connect with people who will help you get where you're going.

- **Week 6:** You'll outline your first product, write a post or create a piece of content that will help you establish your authority and expertise.

- **Week 7:** We'll circle back to look at the things you did in Week 1, and I'll show you how to use the data you've been collecting the last few weeks. You'll submit another guest post proposal and get your site ready to accept payments for your products and services.

- **Week 8:** In your final week, you'll learn some of the social media techniques I've used to promote my writing and build an audience. You'll learn tools, some do's and don't's, and how to use social media to share your content in a way that attracts new clients and grows your business.

After you've worked through Part III, you'll have the complete formula for how I've built a business that reaches thousands of people each month and supports my family. If you want the exit strategy I would deploy if I were transported back to 2012, back to when I was happy at my job but looking for something more, back to before Dave fired me and before I had to figure everything out on my own, this is it.

17: WEEK ONE - THE GROUNDWORK

All you need is the plan, the roadmap, and the courage to press on to your destination.
- Earl Nightingale

A s with most things in life, building your business takes work. You can have it done right, have it done fast, or have it done cheaply. But you can't have all three. Instead of going into debt to open a storefront, this Roadmap will show you how to invest the sweat equity to get it done right and done cheaply, though it may take you a little longer. If you want it done fast, you can drop the cheap and hire someone, but I think it's important to build it on your own.

If you were going to open a bookstore or a restaurant, there are several things you would need to get started. You'd need a location, credit for a loan, inventory to stock the shelves, a kitchen to cook the food, a business plan to woo a bank's loan officer, and the list goes on.

Fortunately for us, the list of things you need to open your online store is much shorter and significantly less expensive.

The four essentials to get started are a domain, a web host, software to create and design your site, and a way to accept payment for your products and services.

We'll scratch the surface regarding domains and hosting during Week 1 of your Roadmap; design and monetization will come later. If you have further questions at any point during the week, I've got a step-by-step walkthrough and a short video of the process at www.ellorywells.com/how-to-start-a-blog. You can also see my recommended tools and resources at the back of this book in Appendix B, but I will share some quick tips for you to keep in mind and some general guidance to help you along the way.

In week one, you'll need to hit the ground running. My guess is you'll need about four hours to get all of these parts done. If you've got distractions to deal with, block out thirty minutes for step one, about an hour and a half for step two, and another couple of hours for step three.

The speed with which you move through these steps will also dictate how quickly you move through the next several weeks. You can move at your own pace, but don't dive in so deep as to get burned out before you even have a chance to get some traction. I know I'm bad about that, and if you're as excited as I was when I started, you run the risk of overloading your brain and getting frustrated.

Go at your own pace. Follow the Roadmap.

Step 1: Domain and Hosting

Your domain is the URL or web address people will go to whenever they want to visit your website. Hosting is the term for the big computer, called a server, which stores all of the images, posts, pages and data you create or upload.

Domain

Your domain is the URL of your website; it's everything between the "www." and the ".com." Your domain should be either your name or the name of your brand. If the name you want isn't available, try adding "the" in front of it. For example, "thejohndoe.com" is better than "john-doe.com".

Your domain shouldn't cost more than $10-$20 unless it has already been purchased by someone else and they're offering it for sale. There are too many ways to modify your name or the name of your brand for you to worry about paying more than $20 for the domain you want. While researching a side project, a broker tried to sell me the URL www.oena.com for $40,000. I laughed, replied with "no thank you," and purchased something slightly different instead.

With the right coupon code, you can get a domain from GoDaddy for $.99. Domain renewals are around $15 per year, so it won't break the bank. If you've never used the 99 cent coupon before, do a Google search for "GoDaddy coupon" and you should be able to find a coupon code you can use.

Tips for Buying a Domain

If you're uncertain about the domain for your blog, use your name. If your name has been taken, try a combination of your first initial and last name or vice versa. Another option is to use your name and a different domain extension like .co, .us, or .net.

- **Length** - The shorter the domain the better. Not only is a short domain easier to remember, but it's also easier to type (especially on mobile devices).

- **Extension** - If at all possible, purchase a .com domain extension. These extensions are easier to remember and go well for your global audience.

- **Domain** - When it doubt, go with your name. It's easy to remember, and it's likely never to change.

- **Spelling** - Don't use funky spelling when picking your domain. Make it easy to type, easy to remember and easy to spell.

Hosting

When you first launch, your hosting plan will be your biggest expense. Don't choose the cheapest host for your site, go with a reputable company with hosting options in the middle of the price list. Expect to pay anywhere from $4 to $7 a month for hosting to get started.

If you have the option, see if you can get a price break by purchasing multiple years of hosting up front. I know the hosting company I use offers a discount of almost 50% to anyone who registers for three years up front. Don't worry; you can cancel your account or move to a new host down the road and get a prorated refund. I have done that, and so have several of my clients.

Tips for Buying Webhosting

Though I didn't start with Bluehost, I moved all of my websites over to their servers about a year after I got started. You can get high-quality hosting through them for about $4 a month if you're willing to pay for three years up front.

- **Location** - Find a host based in your country. Since most of your traffic will come from the country where you live (and where people speak the same language), servers located where you are will serve information faster than servers located an ocean away. If you need help finding a hosting company in your home country, try doing a web search for "hosting companies in [insert your country]."

- **Support** - Before purchasing hosting, call their support team. If the person who answers speaks the same language as you, take it as a good sign. Language barriers will only slow you down in the long run.

- **Chat** - See if your hosting provider has a chat function for their support. When I'm busy, the last thing I want to do is wait on hold for someone to pick up. I'd much prefer waiting on a chat box.

- **Price** - Don't choose the cheapest hosting option out there. I did that when I first started and quickly found that their support was almost non-existent. You should be able to find quality hosting around the $3-$10 a month range, and that shouldn't break the bank.

- **Bulk** - Buying your hosting in bulk can get the price down. Consider signing up for hosting three years at a time to get the bulk discount. Yes, you'll have to pay up front, but the overall price will be significantly lower, and you can always get a pro-rated refund if you decide to switch hosts or shut down your site altogether.

After you register your domain and create a hosting account, it will be time to install WordPress. Whether you choose to create content in the form of a blog or if you only want to sell products from your store, WordPress is your best tool for building your site. Don't let the "Word" in "WordPress" fool you; WP is a fully-featured content management system that powers some of the most popular websites in the world. Plus, the WordPress ecosystems includes hundreds of thousands of plugins - powerful software add-ons that add features, functions and design options to the core WordPress software, many of which are free.

All together you should be able to get your domain and professional hosting for about $150. If you'd rather not pay that much up front, you're in the same spot I was in at the beginning of 2012. I wanted to see if blogging and content creation was something I could stick with and enjoy. Though I wouldn't recommend it, you could register for a free account at www.wordpress.com and see how blogging treats you, though I'm not sure you can run e-commerce through their free plans.

Step 2: Design and Social Media

Designing Your Website

There are many free tools out there to help you build and design the layout of your website, but none of them are as powerful and easy to use as WordPress. Some of the other options may seem easy for beginners, but you'll quickly find services like Wix and Weebly to be somewhat restrictive when you want to change how things look or move things around. I would encourage you to avoid Wix;[9] if not for the reasons I'm about to go into below, then because of its apparent poor performance when it comes to SEO.[10]

WordPress is open source. That means the technology and software that drives it is available for anyone to use and modify. I use and recommend WordPress because there are thousands of free add-ons and additional resources to help you design your website like a pro. There are also free themes you can use to customize the layout, look and feel of your site. And, due to the popularity of WordPress, you're likely to know already at least a handful of people you could call for support if you run into a problem.

I built my very first blog using Weebly because their drag and drop user interface appealed to me as a beginner. However, I

---

[9] "Is Wix good for SEO performance if I'm a small business owner?" via Quora.com – https://www.quora.com/Is-Wix-good-for-SEO-performance-if-Im-a-small-business-owner-How-meticulous-should-I-be-in-choosing-a-website-builder-SEO-wise

[10] "Is Wix Any Good for SEO?" – http://www.brucechant.com.au/is-wix-any-good-for-seo/

quickly found that same interface to be restrictive. I kept running into problems where I couldn't do basic things to change the look of my site. I was hesitant to switch to WordPress, but my friend and owner of Air Tight Marketing (www.airtightmarketing.com), Jason Beaton, finally convinced me to change, and I've never looked back.

After making the switch, I used a free theme for two years before spending $100 to purchase a premium theme from StudioPress.

Another aspect of WordPress that makes it my preferred tool is the ability to use plugins. The plugins, or add-ons, come in two flavors, free and premium. Free plugins can be found at www.wordpress.org/plugins or via your WordPress dashboard under Plugins. Premium or paid plugins can be created by almost anyone, so there's no way to list them all here. However, if you want a complete list of the tools I use and recommend, you can find them at the back of this book in Appendix B or by visiting www.theexitstrategybook.com/appendix-b.

Tips for Designing Your Site

When thinking about the design of your site, remember, less is more. One of the most popular blogs on the internet, www.theminimalists.com has no sidebar, a simple header menu, and almost every image is in black and white. Don't feel like you have to overdo it.

- **Think Mobile** - Over time, an increasing percentage of your visitors will be browsing (and buying) from their mobile devices. Any time you make a change or update your site, be sure your modifications look good and function on phones and tablets, in addition to a normal-sized laptop or desktop.In April 2015, Google began using "mobile-friendliness as a ranking signal. This change will affect mobile searches in all languages worldwide and will have a significant impact on Google search results. Users will find it easier to get relevant, high-quality search results optimized for their devices," which means mobile-friendly sites will rank higher in search results than their non-mobile-friendly competitors.[11]

- **Minimal Menus** - Your website should have a basic menu with no drop downs or sub-headings. Complicated menus don't always function well on mobile devices, and, when they aren't designed well, they are a disservice to your visitors. Tell your audience where you want them to go by showing them a menu on a single line.[12]

- **Speed** - Research shows that people leave slow websites. Visitors do not wait for content to load, and they leave. Slow sites rank lower in Google. Anything you can do to make your site faster, like correctly sizing images and using is usually a good thing to do.

- **Readability** - As our population ages (myself included), small fonts are an increasingly poor choice for your visitors. Choose a font that is easy to read, and at least size 16.

Social Media

One of the most fun parts of blogging and building a business is seeing how your personal network grows. You'll meet new people, make new friends, and discover a world you never knew existed.

To help you accomplish this goal of building a brand and gaining exposure to a broader audience, you'll want to link your new website to all of your social profiles and accounts.

---

[11] Read more about the changes Google made to their search algorythim and why at https://support.google.com/adsense/answer/6196932

[12] If you want to know more about website design and the five essential pages even a beginner website needs, check out my free email course at https://www.ellorywells.com/lp/30-day-blog-transformation/

Also, you'll want to connect your accounts to your site on the backend so you can automatically share your new posts via social media. If you're using WordPress, this can be done easily by activating the Jetpack plugin, turning on the "Publicize" module, and linking your sites that way.

Tips for Your Social Profiles

Consistency is critical when you're building your brand online. And, that consistency applies in particular to your social media outlets. If a visitor to your site, a new subscriber to your email list, or a new client is going to follow you from one social site to another, you should reward them for their efforts. You can do that by creating a consistent experience for your community wherever they may connect with you.

Social media is also an excellent way to add to or enhance the personality of your business. Instead of longer posts via your company or personal blog, social media gives you the opportunity to put your personality (and all of its quirks) on display. Whenever your followers, friends, connections, customers, etc., follow you on social media, they don't do so because they want to be sold to. They follow us because they want to know, like and eventually trust us. And get the occasional special offer.

- **Consistency in Name** - If at all possible, use the same name or brand as your "handle" on every social media site. Your handle is typically everything after the ".com/" for your profile on social media. For example, Gary Vaynerchuk, CEO of VaynerMedia and one of the most influential people on social media today, is a master at social media and branding. On most social networks, you can find him with the username "@garyvee" or by typing "/garyvee" after the URL (ex: instagram.com/garyvee; twitter.com/garyvee). Where there's no URL, like on Snapchat or Periscope, you can find him @garyvee. Since anyone can create a new profile at any time, and there are very few rules about spoofing or copying an account, make things easy for your audience by creating a consistent name/handle across your social profiles.

- **Consistency in Color** - I remember clicking one of the links Pat Flynn shared on Twitter that took me to a landing page for a webinar. I couldn't believe it! Though the landing page was created using LeadPages, the colors used were the same colors Pat uses on his blog.[13] I immediately knew the page was associated with Pat's brand, and I was impressed. As a quick aside, like Gary, Pat is a branding master. He used the same colors, fonts, logos and branding in his presentation that he uses on his website.

- **Consistency in Logo/Headshot** - When your community searches for you online, make it easy for them to identify you by using the same logo or headshot in your profile picture. Don't use a group photo, and don't have a different logo for each site. Consistency is key, and that begins with the first thing people see when looking for you - your profile photo.

- **Use Jetpack** - If you're building your site using WordPress, be sure you install and activate the Jetpack plugin and the "Publicize" module it contains. You can find the Jetpack plugin in your WordPress dashboard or by installing it via the plugins tab. With Jetpack, you can connect a Facebook, Twitter, LinkedIn, Tumblr, Path and Google+ account directly to your website, and each time you publish a new post, a link will be shared to every site you connect.

- **Use Social Plugins** - Sharing your post when you publish it isn't enough. You'll want to use social plugins to make it easy for your readers, visitor, and clients to share something you've created. Tools like the free "Share" tool for the

---

[13] You can find Pat Flynn's website at http://www.smartpassiveincome.com

SumoMe plugin[14] for WordPress will ask you for your social profiles when you're setting them up, so when someone share's your work, you're automatically tagged in the update.

- **Use Social Icons and Buttons** - Not everyone who visits your site is ready to share something, but they may want to connect with you, friend you, or follow you online. By using free plugins like Simple Social Icons by StudioPress,[15] or the "plugin" I created called Better Social Media Buttons,[16] you can add social icons to your website's sidebar. When your visitors click the buttons, they'll find your social profiles and can follow or friend you.

The key to connecting your site to your social networks is to build a community around what you're doing online. People will come for the food, the information, the music, the widgets, etc., but they'll stay and keep coming back for the community   .

Step 3: Analytics and Pixels

While the topics of analytics and pixels aren't the sexiest things to talk about, they're some of the most valuable.

To be honest, I thought about including a section about tracking codes and pixelation in Week 7. I thought it would be better to hold off discussing these topics because they're slightly more advanced and may cause some people to feel overwhelmed.

However, the more I thought about it, the more I realized it would be a big miss on my end to not get these things set up at the very beginning. Instead of waiting for a month and a half and

---

[14] https://sumome.com/

[15] https://wordpress.org/plugins/simple-social-icons/

[16] https://www.ellorywells.com/downloads/social-media-buttons/

missing out on valuable tracking information, data, and statistics, let's get this part knocked out early.

I know you can handle it. If you couldn't, you wouldn't be here, and if you can't, you'll have a hard time building a business. But you've got this! Don't let the idea of copying and pasting code scare you. I'll walk you through it, and we'll do this together.

Google Analytics

Google Analytics (GA) is the default and go to option for getting information about how visitors arrive on your site a what they do while they're there. GA will show you where your visitors come from, how they got you, which pages and posts they viewed while on your site, and which pages made them leave. And it's free.

To get started using GA, go to www.google.com/analytics and either sign in with your Google account or create a new one.

Second, once you've created and verified your account, log into your account and go to the Admin panel. If there's not an Analytics account under the Admin tab, create one using either your name or your company's name.

Third, in the "Property" column, select "Create new property" from the drop-down menu, and then fill out the form on the page that loads. You'll need your website's name, the URL, the industry category for your site, and the reporting time zone (which is the time zone where you're located).

Once you answer those questions and choose your options, click "Get Tracking ID" at the bottom of the page.

On the next page you'll see the Google Analytics Tracking ID that you've been assigned. These IDs typically look like UA-########-#. You don't need to write this down or memorize it, just know that this is a unique identifyer within the GA system. What you're looking for is the "Website tracking" code that will track visitors as they come to your site.

It will look something like this:

```
<script>
(function(i,s,o,g,r,a,m){i['GoogleAnalyticsObject']=r;i[r]=i
[r]||function(){
(i[r].q=i[r].q||[]).push(arguments)},i[r].l=1*new
Date();a=s.createElement(o),
m=s.getElementsByTagName(o)[0];a.async=1;a.src=g;
m.parentNode.insertBefore(a,m)
})(window,document,'script','//www.google-
analytics.com/analytics.js','ga');
ga('create', 'UA-#########-#', 'auto');
ga('send', 'pageview');
</script>
```

Don't worry about what all of those words and symbols mean. I don't know either and it won't matter.

To get tracking results, select the entire code, from the opening < to the closing >, and copy it. If you want to paste it into a text file or Evernote for temporary safe keeping, feel free. Inside your WordPress dashboard, go to the Appearance menu, and click the link for "Editor." You'll need to paste that code your header.php file, or into an analytics plugin, but not both. If you're using StudioPress, go to Genesis and Theme Settings and paste your code in the box titled, "Header Scripts."

Whoa! That wasn't too bad, was it? After you've pasted the code and saved your changes, you should start getting results in Google Analytics within a few hours.

If you can make it through the process of "installing" Google Analytics (and you can), handling Facebook pixels will be a breeze. And, if you can do these two things, most of the technical bits will be behind you, and you can get back to creating content, writing blog posts, shooting videos, recording podcasts, and selling your products and services. In Week 7 we'll look at what we can do with all of the data these tools are collecting.

Facebook Tracking Pixels

At the Thrive conference in Las Vegas in October of 2015, Gary Vaynerchuk called Facebook Ads "the most powerful marketing tool of our time."

What makes Facebook Ads so powerful?

Tracking pixels.

Facebook's pixels will digitally tag everyone who visits your site. Then, when they leave your site and log into Facebook, you can show your ads or updates to them there. In short, you can get in front of your visitors even after they've left your website.

While the steps to create the Google Analytics code hasn't changed much over the past few years, the process of setting up a Facebook pixel has. Overall, the steps are similar to the ones taken to create the GA code, but whereas you only need one code for Google, you can have multiple pixel codes for Facebook.

To create a Facebook tracking pixel, you'll first need a Facebook Page for your business. For reference, you can find mine at www.facebook.com/ellorywells. Once you have a page, you'll need to connect it to Facebook's Business Manager by going to https://business.facebook.com. After you've linked your social and business accounts, you can pay to boost status updates, share videos, and images to your audience.

While I'd love to tell you the exact steps to create a pixel tracking code, I can't. Since I began writing this book, the process has changed several times, and I'm sure it'll change again. But, the Facebook Business Manager tool looks like it's here to stay, and you can find what you need inside there.

However, to get the power of the pixel, you'll have to paste the pixel code into the header section of your site, just like you did for Google Analytics. Facebook's pixel tracking code is a little more complicated and much more frightening to look at so I won't paste it here, but it is incredibly powerful and will allow you to do amazing things with targeted Facebook Ads down the road. Again, we won't get into that until further down the Roadmap, but just know that by adding the code to your site today, you'll be in a much better position later when we're ready to use it.

Step 4: About Page and Post

I learned a long time ago, though I didn't realize it until it was almost too late, that people don't care to read the blogs most businesses like to write. The reason? They suck. And the posts often have no personality behind them.

You're not building another concrete and steel, faceless and heartless company. You're building a business you can love, and that is uniquely your own. If you want a visitor to know, then like, then trust you, you've got to put "you" into every aspect of your business. To accomplish that task, you're going to write a legendary About Page.

Not only is your About Page going to be one of the most viewed pages on your site, but it's also where you can cut loose and have some fun. Whether you blog about leadership, share videos about vegan cooking, or create beautiful black and white photography, your About Page is a place where you can pull back the curtain and tell the world (and your customers) what you're all about.

A good About Page will cover the 5 Ws and the H from before:

- *Who* you are and who your clients are

- *What* you do and what makes you an expert

- *When* you started

- *Where* you learned; where in the world you live; where you are in your journey

- *Why* you're so passionate and why people need you

- *How* you got where you are and how you can help

If you talk about each of these things in detail on your About Page, you'll have no problem building trust with your visitors, followers and customers.

Lastly, use your About Page to showcase your expertise. You don't have to brag or share case studies, but I encourage you to tell a story that illustrates how you figured out your strengths and how you use them to improve the lives of your clients. If you had a life-changing illness that gave you a new perspective on life, share that. If you were fired from your job and realized that you had all of your eggs in one basket and never wanted to lose control again, share that.

Use the words on this highly trafficked page to showcase your skills, share your story, and invite people into your world. Drop the formalities and have a fireside chat with your readers.

After you've written your legendary About Page, use it as an outline to write your first post. Tell the world, "This is who I am. This is why I am here. And this is how I'm going to make this place and the people in it better."

Publish your new post and page, share them on social media, and start asking people to come and see what you're up to!

Congratulations! You now have a domain, the humble beginnings of a website to call your own, and your first post and page to tell your visitors what you're about. Plus, if you made it all the way through Step 3, you'll also start to see where your visitors are coming from, what social sites are sending traffic your way, and what pages they're viewing as they browse your site.

You've just laid the foundation for your business and your success for years to come!

One last thing before we move on.

Over the past few years, I've recorded multiple in-depth training modules for my members and my membership site. I call these video tutorials "Action Plans," and they will walk you through the steps to do much of what you're about to read about. You can get a free 30-day trial membership and gain access to our members' community by going to www.theexitstrategybook.com/offer, and that should give you time to get a good chunk of the way through your Roadmap.

18: WEEK TWO - THE PLAN

I think there's some connection between absolute discipline and absolute freedom.
- Alan Rickman

Now that you've laid the groundwork for your online business, let's start getting some focus and clarity about who it is you're going to serve. In the last chapter, we put things into place that we won't touch for a few more weeks. Let's now outline some of the things you'll be doing to fill in the time between adding the tracking code for Google and Facebook and when you'll start to use it.

When I first started, one of my biggest weaknesses was thinking my products and services were meant for everyone. At the time, if you'd asked me who my target audience was, I would have said, "Anyone who wants to start an online business." For about a year I believed that. And, for about a year, I struggled to connect my message with the people who wanted, and needed, to hear it. If you're trying to reach everyone with your message, you'll end up connecting with no one.

The truth of the matter is, you're not meant to serve everyone. As long as "everyone" is your target market, you will struggle to build your business.

During week two, you're going to look at narrowing your focus by clarifying your avatar. You will develop a content calendar that serves that avatar, that "ideal client." You're going to invite your friends, family, and colleagues to follow you on your journey of entrepreneurship and put a system in place to start capturing the emails addresses that are so crucial to the growth and success of your business.

Step 1: Identify Your Avatar

We'll go over how to find your avatar in greater detail in chapter 30, but for now, let's look at some of the basics. Part of the reason I've delayed the "deep-dive" into your avatar is that what you come up with now might not be what you want to use later down the road. And that's ok.

My avatar changed more than once as my business grew, and I further realized and utilized my strengths. You also may find that the avatar you create and identify today might not be the same avatar that will help you build your business and become your raving fans.

To identify your avatar, think about a particular person who would be a perfect fit for your business. Consider what type of person would gain the most value out of working with you, buying your products, or visiting your store.

Then, think about with who your message would not connect. What type of person would not benefit from hearing what you have to say? Instead of spending time trying to convince someone of the value you bring to the table, you can focus on the people who already see the world as you do.

Tips for Identifying Your Avatar

It may seem like an odd place to start, but when you're trying to identify your avatar, look at yourself. Most times we have to look no further than the mirror when we want to find someone who we can help the most.

- **Solve Your Own Problems** - If you have experienced a problem, the odds are, you're not alone. As you come up with solutions to the problems you're facing, find others with those same problems and help them.

- **People Like You** - Instead of trying to connect and identify with people who aren't like you, connect with people who come from the same place and believe as you do. When you share your story, it will resonate the most with people who've had similar experiences and struggles in life. More often than not, your avatar is a lot like you!

- **Be Specific** - "Men and women between the ages of twenty and fifty" isn't specific enough. Though it's not impossible for a 23-year-old to relate to a middle aged man in his late forties, it's an obstacle you don't need to create for yourself. Instead, try "men and women between 30 and 45 who are newly divorced and who have to figure out how to raise their children in a broken home. One applies to everyone (and, therefore, no one), and the other describes a very targeted cross-section of the population.

- **Create a Profile** - The more you know about your avatar, even if it is an imaginary person, the better you can serve them. You'll eventually know their likes, dislikes, where they shop, what types of things they buy, and what brands they relate to. Once you know those kinds of things, you can meet your avatar where they are and help them in a variety of ways (even the ways that are outside of your core offering).

Again, this is a high-level look at creating your avatar. This is a guidepost to help get you started, not the exact questions you'll want to ask before you can take your impact to the next level. Do this exercise now, and when you get to Chapter 30, you'll be in a much better position.

Step 2: Create a Content Calendar

One of the best ways to take people on a journey is to walk them through it yourself. You can do this with a content calendar.

Using the post types you learned about in Chapter 15, you can create an outline of the types of content you'll produce over the next several weeks and months. If you're a plumber, you could write a "how to" post about finding the most qualified plumber or fixing a leaky faucet. If you are a real estate agent, you could shoot a "top ten" video for YouTube detailing the things to avoid or common mistakes made when buying a home over ten years old. If your goal is to help people save, invest and manage their money, as my friend Amy Robles does, you could write a blog post or record a podcast episode about the questions you should ask yourself before creating a budget. You get the idea.

A content calendar will allow you to plan your audience's journey from where they are to where you want them to be. By putting out free information, you establish yourself as an authority, an expert if you will, on a certain topic.

By the way, each of the examples I just mentioned would be things I would have read, watched, or listened to in the past five years. When our sink was leaking in the kitchen, I went to YouTube and searched for videos about how to fix it. In 2010, when Ashley and I were shopping for a home, we would have welcomed a blog post outlining what to look for, what to avoid, and how to find the best home for our money.

Your content calendar can cover a range of topics and skill levels, but it should always help your readers, viewers, listeners and prospective customers feel like they're getting to know you a little bit better. The content you create should help people feel like they're receiving value from you long before you've asked them for money.

Tips for Creating a Content Calendar

Don't over think it. Your content calendar should reflect your expertise and show your personality. Change it up, have fun, and most of all, be human.

- **Be Consistent** - One thing your audience will want and expect from you is consistency. If you publish posts, videos, or podcasts on Mondays, make sure it's *every* Monday. Think about your favorite lunch spot. Would you keep going if you never knew if they'd be open when you pulled up to the front door? No, you wouldn't. And eventually, you'd stop going. The same principle applies to your website, blog, YouTube channel, and podcast.

- **Be Frequent** - Once a year is consistent, but it's not frequent. Be frequent with your posting schedule, but don't post so often that you can't stay consistent. While a post every day would be great, that rigorous schedule would be hard to maintain. Post as often as you can without degrading the quality of your work.

- **Change It Up** - Don't just write one list post after another. Throw in a "Top 10" or a product review post. While your audience does want consistency, they'll appreciate a little variety too.

- **Share Personal Stories** - In 2012, when I started doing community surveys for my audience, I didn't expect to see "personal stories" show up as one of the things my readers wanted to see the most. If you went to a dinner party, what would you talk about? Most likely you'd share about your family, your kids, the awesome vacation you just went on, and things like that. Sprinkle these personal stories into each bit of content you create, and people will feel like they're a part of your family. When Shane, a fan, came up to me at a conference and asked me how Boomer was doing, I was shocked, to say the least. But, Shane had listened to a podcast episode where I'd mentioned our crazy cat, and asking me about it made him feel like an insider.

- **Think Evergreen** - Evergreen is a term for content that is valuable and relevant for a long time. The opposite of evergreen would be something that focuses on current events or seasonal topics in the news. Evergreen content will help your SEO efforts by drawing visitors to your content for years to come. One of my most popular blog posts, 7 Types of People Successful People Avoid, still gets traffic even though I published it almost three years ago. [17]

I want to reiterate that your content does not have to come in the form of a written blog. If you make custom, hand-crafted cards, your content could be behind the scenes videos of your creative processes. Your "factory tour" could be your workspace where you show off the tools you use to make such beautiful pieces. If you're a chiropractor, maybe your audience would be best served by watching videos about how to avoid pain and injury if you work at a desk all day.

The goal of a content calendar isn't to force you into doing something you don't enjoy. The purpose of planning out your content is to help you cover all the bases and add value to the people

---

[17] Read the post at https://www.ellorywells.com/7-types-people-successful-people-avoid/

who come to see you. So, when they're ready to buy, you're the first person they'll go to for help.

Step 3: Email Friends and Family

Successful people often joke that their first reader, listener, customer, and taste-tester was their mom. For me, this was also true. Our families are there to support and encourage us. In many cases, they're our first mastermind members, our first cheerleaders, and maybe even our first customers. The third task for this week is to email all of your friends, family members, and colleagues and invite them to come see your new website and check out what you're doing.

Think of this as your "soft opening" to work out all of the kinks and issues before you have your "grand opening" for the public. In retail and the restaurant world, this soft opening is a time when you ask the families of your employees to come and check out the new place. You open your doors and invite people in so you can test out your systems. A soft opening is your first test without all the pressure.

Tips for Emailing Friends and Family

If my emails are much longer than a tweet, my own wife says she doesn't always read them. You don't have to fit your "come check out my website" email to 140 characters or less, but I'd suggest you keep it short, sweet, and to the point. You don't want to give them so much information that they have no need to visit your site.

To use an analogy one of my English teachers told me, your email should be like a skirt: long enough to cover the subject, but short enough to be interesting.

Your email should:

- **Be Short** - Keep your email short; no more than three or four sentences. Include the theme of your site, what it's about and that you hope they'll come take a look.

- **Have a Call to Action** - As with everything you write, this email should have a purpose and a call to action. Ask your friends and family to click your link and visit. Ask them for feedback via a reply or via your contact page. But just make sure you ask.

- **Include At Least One Link** - I don't think I can chalk this up to a mistake I've made myself, though I wouldn't be surprised. Be sure you include a hyperlink to your URL within the email. Put it on its own line; bold the text as well. Make sure your link is easy to find and easy to tap or click.

Even if you don't have a lot of people to invite to your site, still invite who you have. And, if they visit your page and give you feedback, be sure you thank them. The people who support you in the beginning will likely be with you and encouraging you for years to come.

Lastly, if your site is in direct competition or conflict with your current job, you might want to skip the email to you boss inviting them to check out your site. As you read from my story, sometimes it's a good idea to keep the two things separate.

Step 4: Email Opt-ins

The final task for your second week is to create a way for your friends, family, and followers to subscribe to get updates and information from you and your website. By setting up an email opt-in form, you can ask the people who visit your site to check out new content your produce, new products you've created, and almost anything else tied to your business.

We'll go into more detail about how to convert visitors into subscribers later in Chapter 28, but for now, the key is getting everything set up. While you may hear about email marketing services costing hundreds of dollars a month, don't worry, there are plenty of free options out there like MailChimp, Mad Mimi, and Benchmark.[18]

My recommendation is to create an account with either MailChimp or Benchmark to get started. After you've created your account, you can either copy and paste the "embed" code provided by them, or you can connect to them via API. Again, don't worry, both of these methods are way easier than they sound.

I won't go into the details because each software option is unique, but what you'll need to do is create a new list (title it "Community" or something like that) and look for the option to share or embed the signup form. Most services walk you through this process immediately after you create a new account, so you should be alright.

Once you have your embed code, paste it into a text widget (under Appearance, Widgets in WordPress) and add it to the sidebar of your site. If you need additional help, there's a great walkthrough at https://codex.wordpress.org/wordpress_widgets.

After you've added your new opt-in form, people who visit your site can type in their email and "subscribe" to the emails you'll start sending in a few weeks. If you've ever heard the famous internet marketing phrase, "The money is in the list," you've now got one!

---

[18] I've personally used MailChimp, AWeber, Benchmark and ActiveCampaign. You can see my list of Top 10 Email Marketing Services by visiting https://www.ellorywells.com/top-10-email-marketing-services/.

Tips for Email Opt-ins

Your email list will be one of the vertebrae in the backbone of your new business. Without it, you're left to connect with your audience, clients and followers via social media, and those avenues are becoming increasingly difficult to use for direct communication.

- **Free** - Don't spend money on your email list in the beginning. Until you have a list of fifty or more, and you have at least a few autoresponders, you'll be just fine with one of the free services I mentioned above.

- **Simple** - Keep your opt-in form simple. A first name and email address is all you need. There is also evidence that you can increase conversion rates (i.e., people signing up) by eliminating the option to add a first name and only requiring an email address. Keep it simple and more people will sign up.

- **Multiple Forms** - One thing many beginners neglect to do is include multiple forms on any given page or post. If you're utilizing a sidebar, add one there and make sure it's "above the fold," or near the top. Also, add an opt-in form in your footer or toward the bottom of your page. This will also lead to more signups and increase conversions.

After you've created your first list and added two or more opt-in forms to your site, save the HTML code for that opt-in form (I keep mine in an Evernote file). You may want to insert it into the posts and pages you'll be creating down the road, and having it saved for convenience will make things faster.

Now you should have a pretty good idea of who you'll be helping with your new business. You've invited your friends, family, colleagues and coworkers to check out your new site. And, you've added a few opt-in forms so you can start capturing email addresses.

It may not feel like it now, but you've now built an incredibly solid (and scalable) foundation from which you can build a business. Anytime you want to start a new site or begin a new business venture, this process will help you do it.

I have done everything in this Roadmap, and these first few weeks are what I wish I'd done at the beginning instead of waiting for a year and a half.

Moving forward, you'll be creating a lot of content and making your site really shine, so if it looks a little rough right now, don't fret. Besides, I bet your site looks better than you think it does, and you're further along than you think you are.

19: WEEK THREE - LOGOS, SEO, AND PLUGINS

Don't be boring... think about your first brand
impression: how can you make it awesomer?
- Scott Edwards

Your website has been constructed. Your avatar has been defined. And your email list is in progress. Now it's time to work on branding, writing, recording, and adding in some of the other tools that will help your website feel like a business.

Building a business is a monumental, incredible and fulfilling task. I've never had more fun, and more frustration, than when working on my website. While I wouldn't wish the headaches on you, I know that as you overcome every obstacle, you'll take even more ownership of your success, and every win you have afterward will be that much sweeter.

Now that you've been at this for a few weeks, how does it feel? Have you begun to see a future full of exciting new possibilities? You may be tired after all of the work you've put in, but, at the same time, I hope you're filled with an enormous passion for what lies ahead.

Step 1: Designing Your Logo

A company's logo is one of the most recognizable parts of its brand. The Nike swoosh, the Coca-Cola font, the Dodge Ram, these are all logos that are recognized around the world. Sports teams put their logos on jerseys and helmets; pizza delivery companies put them on their take-out boxes, and you're going to put yours in your website's header.

If you're like me, you're no graphical designer. I've never used Photoshop, and my logos have always been fairly straightforward. Fortunately for us, there are resources like Fiverr.com and other places we can go to get professional design without spending a lot of money.

Logos don't have to be elaborate or complicated. They can be your initials like IBM; they can be three colorful dots like Asana, or simply a fancy letter E inside of a green circle like mine.

Tips for Logo Design

- **High Contrast** - Your logo may be viewed from a distance or by someone with bad eyesight. Get a logo with clear lines and distinct edges.

- **Black & White** - Even if you have a full-color logo, make sure it looks good and is recognizable in black and white. There may be times when you have to print your logo or have it featured in a magazine, so be prepared.

- **Negative Colors** - I'm not talking about blue being the color of trust; I'm talking about reversing the colors of your logo. If my logo needs to be on a black background, I know black text won't work, so I have my logo's colors reversed with white text instead. You will also want to make sure your logo looks good when whitewashed. All-white and semitransparent logos are good as overlays on videos, so having multiple versions and colors of a logo is a good idea.

- **Think Small** - Your giant logo might be good for a video, but how does it look on a 3.5" screen on a mobile device? Make sure your logo scales both smaller and larger than normal so people don't have to squint to understand it.

- **High Resolution** - This should go without saying, but no low-resolution logos. It's rare, but I still see logos that are blurry. Save your logos in small, medium, and large file sizes so you can scale them as necessary without losing image quality. I have a logo just for a business card sized object so the picture is always clear.

Step 2: Search Engine Optimization

Regardless of what you may have read or heard, SEO is not dead. In fact, it's not only alive and kicking, but it's thriving, growing and spreading.

Whether those analogies made you think about a beautiful vine of flowers or a deadly virus, the fact remains that search engine optimization is just as important today as it has ever been. The mechanics may be different, but SEO is still an important aspect of your business's growth. The good thing is, SEO, or technically the "O" part, is easier today than it's ever been in the history of search engines.

SEO: A Brief, Non-Technical and Somewhat Humorous History

Back in the olden days of the internet, website ownership was not only technical and complicated, but it was also expensive.

In the beginning, if you wanted to tell search engines what your site was about, you had to get your web developer on the phone and ask him to make updates to your content. Since these developers were the only ones with the knowledge to make such changes, they were able to charge site owners a lot of money.

Then, as SEO became more popular, these same developers realized that inbound links were useful for building a site's authority on the internet. The more sites that link back to your site, the better you must be, right? As a result, you could buy backlinks by submitting your domain to a link farm, and, almost overnight, you could go from having ten inbound links to thousands.

Web developers and SEO experts also learned they could trick or try to outsmart the search engines. When they realized a key word or phrase used once could increase traffic, they asked, "Why not use it hundreds of times?" So, SEO gurus and developers who wanted to game the system would code the keyword into the background. They'd overlay white text on a white background, and only the search engines could read it. There was no value to human traffic, just an attempt to target search engines.

Tactics such as these are often referred to as "black hat SEO" and eventually, search engines caught on. Though it took companies like Google, Yahoo and Bing years to figure out a way to combat these black hat tactics, they did. And they did in a big way.

Now, not only is SEO much simpler and free to do, but it's also easier for startups like yours to get significant traffic from search engines. Updates to search engine algorithms practically destroyed any value black hat tactics used to provide and gave a significant boost to sites written for humans.

When Google began making major changes to their search formulas in 2012 and 2013, companies all over the world started to squirm. Small blogs like mine, where we didn't know better, were beginning to get more and more traffic because we were doing things the right way.

The moral of the story is threefold; write to be read, don't try to game the system, and, most importantly, be human.

Tips for Improving Your SEO

Remember the moral of the story, and focus on the person to whom you are writing. Help them. Provide links to relevant resources and information that enhances your message. Building the authority of your site, which we will cover more in Chapter 22 during Week 6, takes time. Play the long game and don't look for a quick fix that will cause you to run for cover the next time some search engine software engineer decides it's time to make another change.

- **Yoast SEO** - One of the first things I install when building any site is the WordPress plugin, Yoast SEO. This free software grades every post and page you publish and makes recommendations to help you improve your SEO score. You can find it by searching in the Plugins tab in your WordPress Dashboard.

- **Use Keywords** - Though black hat tactics are no longer useful, the use of keywords in the text of your post or page is still a good idea. When we read, our eyes scan the page as we scroll down and search for keywords. If we find the keyword we're looking for, we stop and read the paragraph. Plus, when we go to Google to search for something, we also search using keywords. For example, you might search for "Mexican food Round Rock" if you and I were meeting for lunch. Use Yoast SEO to measure your keyword density and shoot for the 2-3% range.

- **Use Key Phrases** - When we search, we typically don't search for the keyword by itself. Instead of "food," we search for "Mexican food." Instead of "best vacations" we might search for "best vacation spots in Texas for $500." These longer key phrases allow us to find exactly what we want instead of what we generally want. If you sprinkle these key phrases into your content, you'll increase the likelihood someone will find your site and find exactly what they're looking for.

- **Use Images** - People love pictures. A picture is worth a thousand words. Instagram, SnapChat, and most of the newest social media sites are focused on using photos and videos. So, if you're writing or creating content for humans who love pictures, use more images in your work. Images draw in the eye and communicate what your message is about.

- **Use Alt Tags** - Not only do images appeal to the eye, but they also provide the opportunity to increase the SEO value of your page through the use of alt tags. These tags can be used to highlight key words or phrases that tell search engines what the image is depicting. An appropriate image that's been properly tagged can do amazing things for your traffic. You can add these relevant key word tags easily in WordPress every time you upload a new image.

Whenever I go in search of a picture to use for a new blog post, I spend, on average, about twenty minutes looking for the perfect picture. Use images that are bold, simple, and powerful.

If you want a list of the sites I use to find images for my posts, I've compiled some of my favorites (all are free), at www.ellorywells.com/can-i-use-this-picture-images-for-your-blog.

Step 3: WordPress Plugins

Regarding WordPress, when it comes to modifying the design and feel of a site, there are two things to consider: themes and plugins. Themes control the overall look, layout, and structure of a site. Plugins, on the other hand, can add new features and functions to an existing theme. You can have a site without plugins, but you can't have one without some sort of theme.

Since there are many plugins I use and recommend, I won't go into much detail here. To find out more about each one, log into your WordPress dashboard, go to Plugins, Add New, and search for the plugin listed below. I suggest you find and install each one so you'll be ready when the time comes.

- **Disqus Comment System** - Better than the default comments option and more powerful.

- **Easy Digital Downloads** - One of the most popular plugins for adding e-commerce to your existing website.

- **Jetpack by WordPress.com** - A bundle of plugins all in one. I disable most of the modules.[19]

- **OptimizePress** - The only premium plugin on this list, OptimizePress helps you create beautiful sales and landing pages with no knowledge of coding required.[20]

- **Pretty Link** - Allows you to turn long, complicated URLS that are ugly into short URLS that are "pretty" and easy to remember. You can also track clicks on your pretty links.

- **Yoast SEO** - Turns almost anyone into an SEO expert. Generates site maps you can submit to Google and Bing.

Over time I've added, removed, and tested hundreds of plugins to help me run my business. I've written about most of the ones mentioned here on my blog at ellorywells.com, and many of these are used to power theexitstrategybook.com as well. These six core

---

[19] For a list of which Jetpack modules I use, go to
https://www.ellorywells.com/wordpress-plugins-business

[20] This is the only plugin in this list that is not free, but it is one that I believe to be critical. To get more info about OptimizePress, go to
http://www.theexitstrategybook.com/optimizepress

plugins will help you generate thousands of dollars in revenue for your business and will help you look like a real professional.

Feel free to play around with and test various plugins to see which ones are the best fits for you and your business. If you find a new plugin browsing through the portal in your WordPress dashboard or by searching https://wordpress.org/plugins, you can feel pretty confident you're getting a safe product. If you're ever curious about what plugins your favorite sites are using, just go to http://whatwpthemeisthat.com, and as long as the site you're looking up is built on WordPress, you'll get a good idea of what plugins are used on that site.

***

From here on out, a significant portion of your time will be spent creating content for your business. Whether that's writing, recording, shooting video, baking cakes, sculpting, or brewing, it's time to invest some serious time putting your skills and expertise on display.

If you're a cook, it's time to start baking, taking photos, and writing down recipes. If you're a real estate agent, it's time to hit the pavement, shoot creative videos, and show why you're the person for the job. If your business is creating custom jewelry, now is when you make as many pieces as you can, take behind the scenes pictures of your workshop, and record a factory tour to showcase your craftsmanship.

Now that you've gotten this far, if you've done everything I've outlined in the first three weeks of the Roadmap, much of your foundation is built. While there will always be more behind-the-scenes work to do, you should be set up and ready to move forward.

I do feel like I should take a moment and offer a word of caution. If you're not enjoying this process, it might be time to either A) take a break, B) start over, C) remind yourself why you're here, or, D) all of the above. This is the stuff businesses are made of. It's not always sexy, it's not always glamorous, but putting in the work when no one is watching is what's necessary for you to win. To paraphrase Jordan Harbinger, the creator of The Art of Charm,[21] if you're not willing to clean the bathroom, you're not cut out to be an entrepreneur.

Fortunately for us, there aren't any toilets in online business. If you're ok with keeping your hands dirty for a while, let's keep going!

[21] http://www.theartofcharm.com

20: WEEK FOUR - CREATE, CREATE, CREATE

Traditional marketing and advertising is telling the world you're a rock star. Content Marketing is showing the world that you are one.
- Robert Rose

Creating content in your business is the process of taking your prospective clients on a journey. Your posts, videos, factory tours, and how to material is how you will walk people through the process of getting to know you, learning to like you, and feeling like they can trust you.

Instead of paying for celebrity endorsements, we're going to employ what would get Mark Cuban's attention on Shark Tank: straight hustle. As the saying goes, entrepreneurs are the only people who will spend eighty hours each week working for themselves, so they don't have to spend forty hours working for someone else.

Now that the back end, behind the scenes, and administrative things are largely out of the way, it's time to put our noses to the grindstone and get to work creating the content that will turn prospects into leads and leads into paying customers.

In this chapter, there are three tasks: create content, download and use my blog post idea web tool, and create more content. I've divided it up like this because I want you to write, record, cook, film and produce as much content as you can, up to and including the point at which you run out of ideas. Next, using the tool I'm going to give you, you can turn one idea into several more, and begin creating a web of content that will keep your audience engaged for hours. Then, finally, it's time to create more material using the ideas generated during step two.

This method, if used correctly and repeated over time, will help you create a never-ending supply of ideas which you can use to create a plethora of content to help you market your business   .

Step 1: Create Valuable Content

Every conversation you're a part of can be the seed of content creation. If someone asks you about the process you use to weed out all but the best job candidates, you can create a checklist or training video documenting the process. When your mom says, "I really have no idea what you do," take that as an opportunity to record a behind the scenes video or add to the About Page you created in Week 1.

Once you train your brain to be on the lookout, every comment, question, Facebook group post, Buzzfeed video or Quora question can be the spark of an idea. There are people everywhere asking questions to which you have the answer; you just have to find them and be willing to provide value without asking for anything in return.

Tips for Creating Valuable Content

As I mentioned, content ideas are everywhere. Let's take a look at some ways you can fill your content calendar with blog posts, videos and other types of material people want to read and consume.

- **Take Notes** - I can't tell you how many of my blog posts and videos have come as a result of a conversation. Explaining things to my wife, coaching a client, and answering questions from friends and colleagues have all led to content other people have found valuable. Keep an Evernote file full of topic ideas. Each new note can be turned into a new post.

- **Solved Problems** - If you've solved a problem for yourself, why not share how you did it with your audience?

- **Use Templates** - Use the content types I listed earlier in Chapter 15 and create each one of those posts.

- **Reddit** - Go to www.reddit.com/search and look for topics related to your business or industry. Take note of the questions being asked and the solutions provided. Create a piece of content that either answers the top questions from your search or compiles a list of the top ten answers. Rinse and repeat.

- **Quora** - Go to www.quora.com, create an account, and follow the same process as above.

- **Think, "What Else?"** - The most successful companies are the ones that create ecosystems and communities around their products or services. What else is causing your avatar to struggle? What else do they need help with? What else do they have questions about? Find out; then figure out a way to help. (Example: You may only sell hand-made soaps, but your customers will also need to buy shampoos, scrubs, exfoliants, perfumes, etc. Think about what else they'll need to buy and help them buy it so they can get the most value out of your solution.)

If you're having trouble coming up with new ideas for content, pick up the phone and call one of your existing customers. If you don't yet have customers, get in contact with someone who's read your content, sampled your products, or is aware of your goal. Ask them how they like what they purchased from you. Ask them how (and if) they're using it. See what else they purchased to go along with what they bought from you.

Think about it. We don't only buy jackets when it's cold; we need toboggans, gloves and scarfs too. We don't just buy books; we grab new highlighters, bookmarks, and journals to go along with them. The ecosystems that surround our products are out there if we're willing to look for them. When you can create the product and influence the ecosystem, your profits will soar, and your clients will reward you. Memorable experiences are much more profitable than simple monetary exchanges.

Step 2: Use the Blog Post Idea Web

Back in 2014, I realized how much overlap there was in my content. I wasn't creating the same material over and over, but I was creating an interconnected web of posts that linked to one another and increased the value I had to offer.

When I realized this network of blog posts, podcast episodes and videos was keeping visitors on my site longer, boosting my overall influence and authority, and enhancing my domain authority, I started to see if other people were doing the same things. Some of the big players were, but most people were not intentionally creating a content network that would keep readers engaged.

So, to help my readers then, and to help you now as you begin your content creation efforts, I created my Blog Post Idea Web, which you can download completely for free by going to www.theexitstrategybook.com/ideaweb and entering your best email address.

Tips for Getting the Most Out of the Blog Post Idea Web

You may want to dog ear and come back to this chapter after you've published a few posts and determined what content has gotten the most traction with your audience. Though you don't need to have a library of existing content when you begin working on the idea web, it helps.

- **Original Topic** - Begin with your original topic idea in the middle of the page. If you have a particular post, video, etc., that has done very well, use that one first.

- **Secondary Topics** - Work your way out from the middle. What questions run parallel to the original? What point of view contradicts your first idea? If your original topic was "for" a cause, how could you convince the people who are against it? If you have a Top 10 in the middle, could you create a Bottom 10 or Top 10 Worst post?

- **Tertiary Topics** - After you've created a web of secondary topics, what other ideas have you come up with? Even if they're not directly related, write down these thoughts too.

Every time I've done this exercise with the blog post idea web, I've come away with more ideas than I can create content about. One of the key elements to the success of this exercise is to link from your original idea to the new ones that support it or contradict it later. Don't forget to go back to the initial post or video and add the links to the new material.

Sometimes I refer to this process as "cross-pollination." It's taking one idea and spreading it around to generate new ideas and content, and it helps your visitors remain engaged longer.

Step 3: Create More

Wouldn't it be nice if we could create one incredible piece of work and then relax for the rest of our days? Sure, that may sound good, but that only works for 19th-century painters and other artists who weren't recognized for greatness until after they were dead.

Any company who wants to be successful has to continue innovating, inventing, and producing amazing products long after they feel like doing it. Using the Blog Post Idea Web and the templates from Chapter 15, create as many blog posts, Instagram photos, YouTube videos, SnapChat stories, Periscope scopes, Blab blabs, and tweets for Twitter as you possibly can. Don't dilute the impact of your message by putting out mediocre content, but share your best work with the world. Tell us how you've got the glass of water we're looking for and we'll come see if it's true.

Create, create, and create some more. Push the limits. If it makes you feel uncomfortable, write about it, record about it and share about it. Your success will be found beyond your comfort zone.

How does all of this sit with you? Is it more or less work than you imagined? Have the last few weeks been invigorating or exhausting? This is the life of an entrepreneur, and I welcome you to it!

If you feel like you could use some encouragement, or if you'd just like to share what you've been working on, please feel free to email me at ellory@ellorywells.com. I'd love to hear from you and see how your exit strategy is shaping up!

21: WEEK FIVE - GOING OUTSIDE

A great band is more than just some people working
together. It's like a highly specialized army unit, or a
winning sports team. A unique combination of elements
that becomes stronger together than apart.
- Steven Van Zandt

Nothing great has ever been achieved by a single person acting alone. Even in the "solo" sports of golf and cycling, the successful athletes we see on television have surrounded themselves with a group of advisers, mentors, coaches, and even other players. Without their team, these "solo" athletes would ultimately fail. If you want to be great, you'll be required to surround yourself with great people. In Week 5, I'm going to help you do that!

This chapter is called "Going Outside" because up to this point, much of your work has been behind closed doors, literally if not at least figuratively. But, if you're going to make the impact on the world that you want to make, it's going to take you going "outside," making introductions, meeting new friends, and getting exposure for what you're working on.

To help you accomplish this task of reaching out and making a connection, I've outlined three new tasks which will help you tremendously.

Step 1: Guest Appearances

In the blogging world, guest appearances have historically meant guest "posting." This is usually when you'd write a blog post and ask another blogger or editor if they'd allow your content on their website. While this is still an excellent way to get your message in front of a new audience, guest appearances have taken on an entirely new meaning due to the growing popularity of streaming video.

But, before we go into some of the more recently added ways to do a guest appearance, let's look at the tried and true method of guest posting.

Benefits of Guest Posting

Having your content featured on another website will help you get exposure to new audiences. It would be like radio stations in other cities picking up your show and syndicating it across the country.

On your site, you may target your ideal avatar, the particular type of person who your message would connect with the most and who would get the greatest value from what you have to offer. The sites you guest post on can help you reach people just to the left or right of "ideal." Sharing your content on other sites will help you get your message in front of people who might not otherwise have a chance to see it.

When I survey my readers each year, there's always a significant portion who say they found me through a link on someone else's site.

Other Types of Guest Appearances

Nowadays, practically everyone has the ability to record and stream video from their cell phones. These tiny devices are like professional studios right in our pockets. Regardless of whether or not you use your mobile device to record or stream, you can still take advantage of guest appearances through co-hosting a podcast, showing up to the "studio" of your friend's YouTube channel, or sharing status updates on Twitter, SnapChat or Instagram when you're together.

Too often we forget to have a little fun when starting, building or growing our businesses. Guest appearances are an occasion to pull back the curtain a little bit and share our personalities with new people. Particularly, in the beginning, use every chance you can get to put your message in front of new eyes and ears. Each person you can include in your status update, video, photo or event is an opportunity to exponentially expand the reach of your message.

How to Book Guest Appearances

Your task for step one this week is to book at least one guest appearance. At this point, it won't make much of a difference if it's a guest post on a blog or a co-host spot on a podcast or YouTube channel, the benefits are about the same. Your goal is to connect with at least one person who will help you get your name out there.

If your business is offline, don't worry, there are ways you can do this too. For example, if you're a real estate agent, you could host a lunch and learn with your favorite mortgage broker or homebuilder and invite prospective buyers, sellers, or even other agents from your office. Also, don't forget that even if your business is offline, your customers, future business partners, investors, etc. are online. You can, and should, still share your experiences and stories on a podcast episode or video blog.

When you think in terms of collaboration instead of competition, the world will look a little different to you, and you'll begin to see opportunities all over the place.

It doesn't matter if you reach out via phone, text, email or social media. If the first attempt doesn't work, try another; sometimes people are more in tune with their Facebook messages than they are with their email inbox. If they don't respond within a few days, don't take it personally, but do follow up. We all get busy, and even the most well-intentioned people forget to respond sometimes. Here are a few other things to keep in mind.

- **Think Win/Win** - When approaching someone about a guest appearance, think about what you have to offer them and their audience. You do have expertise and your message has value, but why should they care if you want to be a guest on their site or co-host an event with them? Lead with how you can help them achieve their goals.

- **Be Personal** - It's ridiculous how obvious it is when I receive messages that are copied and pasted to dozens of people at the same time. When I get a message like that, I almost never respond. Personalize your message to the person to whom you're reaching out.

- **Be Current** - One of the best "pitches" I have ever received was from the owner of Plum Deluxe, Andrew Hayes. Though his introductory email started out like hundreds of others I've received, he added in just enough current and personal information for me to believe he wanted to be on my show. In his "P.S." he even left a comment related to something I'd been discussing on my Facebook page earlier that day. I was thoroughly impressed, and if you do something similar, when you reach out for a guest appearance, your prospective host will be too.

- **Have a Plan** - If you're going to request a guest appearance, have a plan for what will happen if they say "yes." Instead of saying, "Let's do something together," present them with a plan of action. Instead, try "Let's host a lunch meeting together next month where we can meet each other's clients and both have the opportunity to share how we can help them." If you lead with a plan, your potential host will be much more likely to say yes or, at least, counter with something equally beneficial.

- **Be Specific** - The more specific you can be about how you can contribute to the guest appearance, the better. If your message is in perfect alignment with or is complementary to the person you're reaching out to, you'll be much more likely to get a response. However, be aware of how you present yourself and your business; don't describe your guest appearance in a way that could be interpreted as an attempt to steal clients. They will likely be skeptical in the beginning anyway, so be clear that you're looking to work together for a mutually beneficial outcome.

Finally, don't be nervous. If you're an introvert like me, guest appearances and the veteran outreaches I'll share about next can feel awkward and uncomfortable. However, if you're going to start a business, not to mention grow a successful one, you've got to reach out and connect with people. If you're not an introvert yourself, try to find one to connect with. As Susan Cain wrote in her bestselling book *Quiet: The Power of Introverts in a World That Can't Stop Talking,* introverts are some of the smartest, most intuitive people you'll find and can be great partners in business. Partner with someone who brings out a different side of you and who shares your vision.

Whether through a podcast interview, a guest post, or a recommendation, these types of guest appearances have contributed greatly to the spread of my brand and the success of my business.

Step 2: Veteran Outreach

Where the guest appearance is meant to connect you with someone on the same level, at the same stage of business, or who's business could be complimentary to yours, this step is meant to get you connected with a veteran in your niche. Your goal here is to find at least one person who is already doing today what you'd like to be doing in a year, two years, or even ten years down the road. Despite our desires to be unique with our businesses, there's always someone out there we can learn from. And, there is almost always a company out there with a business model that's worth looking at a little closer.

When I started my blog in 2012, as I've mentioned, I had no idea what I was doing. I also didn't really know how to get started, attract readers, build an email list, create and sell products, do SEO or any of the other things I'm teaching you in this book.

What I did have were veterans I learned from and leaned on heavily. Bloggers like Pat Flynn and Michael Hyatt were my go-to veterans who I looked to almost daily for ideas, inspiration, example and advice. Though I never reached out to them in the way I'm recommending to you, I did meet both of them in person early on in my journey. Even if I hadn't had the opportunity to shake their hands, I still would have learned from them. I would have used their websites, business models, and content calendars as the framework for how I'd build my business. And that's exactly what I did.

Tips for a Successful Veteran Outreach

Every industry is different. Therefore, the veterans in your business will likely not be the same ones whom I'd reach out to. As a side note, connecting with veterans *outside* your industry would be a great thing to do! Use these tips to connect with the veterans both inside and outside of your typical circle.

- **Be Honest** - Veterans can smell a "pitch" from a mile away. After you've been pitched a few times, you too will begin to notice the signals. Avoid sounding warning bells, and be honest with the veteran you're reaching out to. Don't try to hide the reason why you're reaching out.

- **Be Humble** - When was the last time you wanted to help an arrogant person?

- **Be Direct** - Veterans are busy; that's why they've survived so long! If you have a question, ask it. If you'd like to have coffee, make sure that's clear. Don't beat around the bush. It will only be seen as a waste of time.

- **Have Something to Offer** - Think about what value you can bring to the conversation. It might be tough, but don't approach someone with your hand out. Consider promoting one of their products (you must love it first) without asking for something in return. If your veteran is an online personality, a blogger, podcaster, radio host, etc., consider sharing their material on social media for a few weeks to "get on their radar."

- **Do Your Research** - Approach your veteran armed with knowledge about what they're up to or what they're working on. Using a strategy similar to the one Andrew Hayes used with me, you can show that you're interested in the veteran instead of looking like you've sent the same email or made the same phone call to hundreds of people.

Veterans are people too. Show them that you cared enough to personalize your call or email, and you'll increase your odds of getting a response   .

Step 3: Email Your List

It's now been a few weeks since you first emailed your friends and family members about your new business venture. How did that go? Did anyone sign up? If not, don't worry. I don't think my mom signed up at first either.

However, if you've written a great About Page, created valuable content, and made quality contacts with other people in your industry, the odds are you've picked up a few subscribers by now. If you have, it's time to email them.

The keys to emailing your list are to add value, be relevant, and connect on a human level. Some studies show that over 80% of all email sent is spam and it's your goal to get your emails read.

In this first official email to your list, also called a broadcast or a campaign, I want you to share what you've been working on and provide a link so your subscribers can check out your work.

Tips for Emailing Your List

While the content of your emails will change, some will be promotional, others will be informational, the tactics and strategies will largely remain the same.

- **Use an Email Marketing Service (EMS)** - Not only is it required by the Federal Trade Commission to include certain links in your emails, but it's also good manners. An EMS like ActiveCampaign or MailChimp will always insert all of the required links and information into every email you send. Plus, you can't use your personal email, like Gmail, Outlook or Yahoo, for emailing your list. It's a big "no no." After you send a certain number of emails, these companies will start taking a closer look and could stop you from sending altogether. And, sending emails with everyone in the BCC field is a dead giveaway that you're not sending a personal email.

- **Have a Compelling Subject Line** - Your subject line is the first thing your subscribers will see when your email hits their inbox. A compelling subject line should tell them enough to make them want to open the email and read what's inside. A quality headline should also be relevant to the topic of the email and give the reader an idea of what's inside. Seem like common sense? You'd be surprised (or maybe you wouldn't!).

- **Address Recipients by Name** - Nobody wants to receive an email that starts, "Hey Subscriber!" or "Dear Friend." Most email service providers allow you to customize your emails through merge tags or personalization tags. These automatically insert custom information based on the recipient of the email. For example, if you're using MailChimp, you could use the merge tag *|FNAME|* to insert someone's first name. If you don't have someone's first name, or if you haven't been capturing them via your opt-in form, just leave it off and try to sound natural. Do your best to write your emails to subscribers just like you'd write an email to a friend. Because I use ActiveCampaign's merge code to insert someone's first name with the first letter capitalized, most of my emails start out, "Hey %FIRSTNAME|UPPERFIRST%!" - just like I'd begin an email to a friend I wanted to meet for lunch.

- **Include Multiple Links** - Include a link or call to action at the beginning, middle, and end of your emails. Statistically, the first two links in your email will get the most clicks, but you can't leave it at that. Including multiple links in your emails will increase your click-through rates significantly.

- **Be Natural** - As I mentioned above, write your emails to your subscribers like you'd write an email to your friends. Write like you talk.

- **Think Mobile** - Like when you're designing your site, it's equally important to think about mobile users when writing your emails. Well over 70% of my subscribers read my emails on a mobile device. What would be a short paragraph on a full-size screen can easily become a wall of text on a phone. Use no more than two sentences per paragraph and keep those sentences brief.

- **Test** - Many email marketing services allow you to send test emails or preview messages on mobile devices before sending them to your list. I test every email by sending it to myself, at least three or four times, before I send it to everyone else. I check for spelling errors and formatting issues, both on my computer and on my phone. As they say, you only have one chance to make a first impression, so make sure your carefully crafted email is exactly like you want it.

- **Don't Use Big Images** - If you were emailing your friend, would you put a big image right in the middle of it? No. At most, you'd attach it as a file. The same principle applies to your email marketing efforts. Plus, big images are one thing that will trigger the spam filters on most email service providers like Gmail.

- **Test Against Spam Filters** - Some email marketing services allow you to test your emails against their spam filters before you send them. Before I send an email, I try to get my emails to a spam score of 0.0.

- **Send on Schedule** - Email your list with consistency and regularity. Once a year is consistent but not frequent enough. Your subscribers opted-in because they want to hear from you; they gave you permission to email them, so be sure you do! Studies show that three to four emails a month is about as infrequent as you should get. Much more time in between and you risk people forgetting who you are and why you're emailing them in the first place.

Email marketing can be tricky. No one has all of the right answers and sometimes it's a constant battle to get into the inbox. It's not a bad idea to direct new subscribers to an "email whitelisting" page with instructions on how to make sure they get your emails. You can find my email whitelisting page and instructions on my site at www.ellorywells.com/email-whitelisting and use it as an example. After all, if your emails don't get into the inbox, they're likely to not get read at all.

Week 5, Going Outside, is all about connecting with people. Whether those people are your customers, prospects, business partners or the veterans who can help you on your journey, you'll need to get outside of your home office or the workshop in your garage and build a network of people to help grow your business.

Try getting a new guest appearance scheduled at least once per month. Reach out to a new veteran every quarter or every six months so you're always expanding your network. Email your subscribers once a week to keep your list warm. Though we won't talk much about these activities in the rest of your Roadmap, you should keep these tasks on your to-do list until you retire.

22: WEEK SIX - BUILDING INFLUENCE

The key to successful leadership today is influence, not authority.
- Ken Blanchard

Influence comes in two flavors - the kind you build and the kind you borrow. If you're going to be successful in business, you'll need to do both. There is no other way to become influential, and both ways are equally effective.

All along we've talked about how getting people to know, like, and trust you is the key to selling, business building, and success. At each of those stages, you establish your expertise and create a certain level of influence over the people who may buy from you. You influence them to consider working with you, or, you influence them to trust that you can do what you claim. Without influence, most efforts, in any area of life, will ultimately come up short.

One of the objections I often hear from aspiring entrepreneurs is that they aren't an expert at anything. If you're struggling to build influence and establish yourself as an authority in your industry, you may feel the same way.

But the good thing is, it isn't as hard as you may think. In fact, in today's modern, connected world, becoming an expert is easier than perhaps ever before in history. And, once you realize that finding someone to sell to is just a matter of finding someone who needs what you have, you'll be open to a new world of possibilities.

So, then, the problem becomes one of building enough influence to get things done. Influencing a team to help you out; influencing a prospective buyer to sample your products; influencing someone to invest their time, money, or resources with you.

For the purposes of this chapter, let's use the terms credibility, authority, and influence interchangeably. Influence is your ability to exert authority over someone. Credibility is when someone believes and has faith in your authority. In a way, influence is the act of using your authority and credibility to make things happen. Though different, they are similar enough for our purposes.

Your job during Week 6 is to create two pieces of content, a research post, an authority post, and begin working on a $10 product.The first two tasks will help you build and borrow influence, and the third will help you take advantage of that influence when the time is right.

Step 1: Your Research Content

Expertise comes from having more knowledge than the people around you. If you have more knowledge and you know how to apply it, you have influence.

For example, an Eagle Scout may be a camping expert amongst people who have never camped before, but a relative novice when in the company of Army Rangers or other Eagle Scouts.

On the other hand, expertise comes from having specialized skills, knowledge other people don't have, or hours of training and practice.

If expertise comes from being smarter than the next guy, the bar is set pretty low. According to a study by YouGov and the Huffington Post, 81% of people surveyed had read zero "nonfiction books, such as history books or how-to books" in the last twelve months. [22] The fact is, most people do nothing to improve themselves after they walk the stage at graduation.

The stats don't get much better for readers of fiction. 70% of people hadn't read a novel either. On top of that, 28% of individuals surveyed hadn't read a single book at all. No bestsellers, no thrillers, no bathroom books while you're sitting on the throne - nothing.

So, if you spend just one hour during the year focused on personal development and learning about your topic of choice, you'll have more "expertise" than seventy percent of the people walking the streets.

Being better than the worst isn't good enough, not if you're going to build a successful business and sell what you know. If you're going to stand out as an expert, you have to be the best of the best. You can't just be better than 70 or 80% of the world; you have to be better than 99% of it. Luckily, you can get there with an investment of time and energy. Reading books and learning is one of the best ways to help you become an expert, and when you share your knowledge, you build influence

The purpose of a research post or video is to show the people in your audience that you know what you're talking about. I don't say this to imply your customers are distrusting. But, a research post can show your expertise, enhance your credibility and boost your influence in a very effective way.

Let me give you an example.

A few years ago, my wife and I went to Fredericksburg, Texas. We wanted to see what the buzz was about and why this part of Texas was the second most popular wine destination in the country.

---

[22] https://today.yougov.com/news/2013/09/30/poll-results-reading/

At one of the vineyards, we decided to pay a little bit extra and go on the cellar tour. The sommelier took us through the vineyards and into the barrel rooms, and we completed the tour in a private tasting room where we had the opportunity to taste the same wine aged in three different types of barrels. On this tour, we met fantastic experts across several parts of the winery's business and even got to see the equipment used to de-skin the grapes and turn them into pulp.

Even though the other aspects of the winery's business, like the marketing, the street appeal, the customer service, etc., had already influenced us to make a purchasing decision, the cellar tour enhanced that influence and convinced us to become wine club members. To the tune of hundreds of dollars a year, this winery gets our business almost exclusively.

Instead of writing a research "post," the winery put their knowledge, expertise and unique style on display. Instead of creating a video for YouTube or a podcast for iTunes, they offered an in-depth participatory experience where tourists could taste the different processes and procedures used to make fantastic wine.

As I've mentioned before, you don't have to be a writer to apply these strategies to your business. The tactics you employ are important and they can also be tailored to your particular business, industry, or niche.

Step 2: Your Authority Content

While you should always be reading and learning, there are other ways you can establish yourself as an expert. One of these tactics uses your direct experience with producing results. The other comes from association and should only be a supplement to the reading and studying you're doing on the side.

There are two types of Authority Posts, and both are designed to establish your expertise. The first is the *look-at-what-I've-done-*

and-here's-how-I-did-it type of post where you have an opportunity to brag a little bit about your accomplishments. The second is the *here-is-what-I-know-and-the-collective-knowledge-of-experts* post where you gain authority based on the elite and expert crowd with which you associate. The first piece of content is building your authority, the second is borrowing it.

"Look What I've Done"

To quote Jim Rohn, "Results are the name of the game." If you can produce results, people will see you as an expert. And, when you share the results of your efforts with your audience and help them achieve their goals with the information you've shared, you will have influence.

When it comes to building influence and establishing yourself as an expert whom people come to for advice, what it all boils down to helping people solve problems. Do that often enough and solve enough problems, you'll be able to influence the members of your audience to take a variety of actions, including making buying decisions.

Your "Look at What I've Done" authority post, video or factory tour is your chance to brag. This is your opportunity to show the world the results of all of your hard work, your patented procedures, and the value of your unique selling proposition. If there was ever a time to say, "I'm awesome and here's the proof," this is it.

However, as we know, anyone can put anything on the internet; just because you read it online doesn't make it true. That's where the rest of the authority post comes in. The second half, which is equal in importance to the first, is where you illustrate how your efforts led up to the positive result.

Like the winery where my wife and I are members, if you've won awards for your product, now is the time to pull back the curtain and show us how you did it. You don't have to give away corporate secrets to show why your process leads to great results.

The way you hand-craft your widgets, the precision with which you prepare your meats, the attention to detail you put into your jewelry, all of these things illustrate your effectiveness, help justify your results and boost your authority and influence.

"Look What I Know"

While the previous example is a direct play at building your authority, the "Look What I Know" post is a way of borrowing it. When we stand on the shoulders of giants we become giants ourselves. And this rubbing of the shoulders with the elites will help you be seen as an elite yourself.

By associating with other experts, you'll also be seen as an expert. You can gain expertise by writing blog content and having it published on larger websites and publications. These guest posts not only build your site's authority and improve search engine optimization, but they also give you credibility and expertise to everyone who reads your content. If the editors at Entrepreneur Magazine deem your post worthy of sharing with their audience, you'll gain expertise simply by being associated with their brand.

Another way to come up with material for a "Look What I Know" piece of content is to survey the top people in your field, ask them all the same questions, and compile the results. You could do video interviews, show yourself on camera with each expert and share "exclusive" insights. You could conduct email surveys, collect the responses, and curate the best responses into a technical white paper or blog post.

Popular internet business coaches like Jaime Masters of Eventual Millionaire and John Lee Dumas of Entrepreneur on Fire have built their entire business around being associated with other experts. Both Jaime and John interview guest experts for their podcasts and share the wisdom they receive with their audiences.

The cool thing is, the "Look What I Know" tactic requires only that you ask questions to the right people, not that you spend days, weeks or even years doing all of the research yourself.

If you want to take this strategy to the next level, consider the questions your audience and customers might have, survey the experts with the questions you expect people will have, and then deliver their responses. If you can predict the challenges your audience will face, when they encounter those challenges, and you're right there with the answers, they'll think you're a genius.

I believe you know by now that you must have substance to back up your authority posts and that you'll need other types of authority-building tools if you want to be truly successful. But, if you follow up your major successes with a "Look What I've Done (and Here's How I Did it" kind of post, video, or documentary, you'll be carrying the momentum of your win far into the future. Combine that with the occasional survey of experts, and you've got a content calendar to envy.

Step 3: Your $10 Product

Before starting a company to manufacture and supply piston rings for Toyota, Soichiro Honda fixed cars. Before that, he apprenticed as a mechanic. And, even before that, Honda helped his father repair bicycles in their village at the base of Mount Fuji.

Long before Soichiro founded the Honda Motor Company, he was tinkering in the shop, working with his hands, and even making fake stamps for his fellow students so they could falsify their family seal on unfavorable report cards. Soichiro's life-long passion of working with engines and oil turned into one of the most successful car companies of all time.

Honda's success, from the very beginning, was not due to good grades or a prestigious education. In fact, Honda never received a formal education before he left home at the age of fifteen. His success was due to two things: the fact that he dedicated his time to improving his craft, and he took small wins and leveraged them into much larger opportunities.

The boy who used the melted rubber of a bicycle pedal cover to forge rubber seals turned his passion for engines and oil into a company that made the best-selling motorcycles in the entire world. It all started with the small, albeit unethical, taste of entrepreneurship Honda received as he sold fake family seals to his friends from the school yard.

Give people a sample of your capabilities and leverage the experience into larger opportunities. Don't worry about knocking it out of the park on your first step up to the plate. Learn from everything you create and continue getting better. It worked for Soichiro Honda; it worked for Mark Zuckerburg; it worked for Steve Jobs, Elon Musk, Dave Ramsey, Oprah Winfrey and Howard Schultz, and it'll work for you.

That's why I recommend starting with a $10 product.

While your $10 product probably won't make you rich, there are several benefits to creating and selling a lower-priced item. Think of your product like a $10 business card; it tells people about who you are, what you stand for, and how you can help the world.

You can't give it away for free because people don't value what they get for free; people will take free samples all afternoon at Costco without buying anything. But, your $10 product will provide both you and your customers with a tremendous amount of value. Here's why:

1: Your product tells the world who you are.

When you're first starting out, no one knows you or your business. We may stumble upon your blog or walk into your business because one of our friends shared a link on Facebook, but we still don't know you.

Your $10 product is the world's gateway to your beliefs and what you stand for. It shows your customers what you're about and what you believe in, whether that's something spiritual or more literal, like your attention to detail and dedication to quality.

Think about your product as a test drive, and your coaching program, training series, wine club membership, etc., as the whole car. Would you buy a car without test driving it first? I know I wouldn't. Your $10 product gives people a glimpse at a possible future. One filled with self-fulfilment, adequate knowledge, or quarterly wine shipments; a future they may want more of down the road.

2: Your product is a stepping stone.

At a $10 price-point, your product is obtainable without requiring people to risk too much financial capital. Not everyone can afford a $500 product, and not everyone wants to, especially if they don't know you.

I don't know about you, but I'm often willing to spend $10 to test something knowing full well that if it doesn't work, I didn't lose much. Though that's not the attitude you want to have when *creating* the product, it's a fair enough way of thinking when *buying* the product. Ashley and I were comfortable spending $8 on a glass of wine before spending $30 on a tour that turned into $500 a year on a wine club membership.

By releasing a $10 product, you are able to add value to your audience, community, and customers without creating a high monetary hurdle. Plus, if customers love your ebook, album, workbook, etc. that you offer for $10, they're much more likely to buy the course, the concert ticket or the membership program for a couple hundred.

Let me give you another example that involves one of my favorite things to do - reading spy-thriller fiction novels.

When I first discovered the books of the late Vince Flynn, I didn't buy the whole series at once. I sat in an over-sized lounge chair in Barnes and Noble and read the first ten pages of each of his first three books for free.

Did I want to spend a hundred dollars and purchase every book Vince had ever written? No. I wanted to see if I liked his style of writing, his characters, and the world he'd created with his books.

After taking my free samples, I bought Flynn's first three books that day, and over the next several years I bought every book he'd ever written. I joined his legion of loyal fans, and it all started with a $7.99 paperback. Your $10 product will achieve the same thing. It will provide a stepping stone to the full array of the goods and services you have to offer.

3: Your product is a quick win-win.

A sale at $10 is sometimes easier than a sale at $50, and a quick sale is a quick win. Putting together a product that sells for $10 often takes about a month, less if you really hustle.

By investing the time to put together a short ebook or sample of your music or video series, you're creating something people want. They want to read your guide, they want to hear your music, and they want to see your video training. In the "offline" sense, they want to sample your food, taste your new brew, or experience the quality of your craftsmanship.

When someone buys your introductory product, they get the value of enjoying what you've created, and you get the value of their hard-earned dollars. Win-win.

In this regard, your $10 product is like the sample of orange chicken you get at the food court at the mall. Just when you start to think you can wait until you get home to eat, Panda Express is wafting the smell of their noodles and sauce, and offering you a taste of the freshly fried chicken.

You get a sample of what they have to offer, and they get the possibility of taking your money. In the food court, you have a need, and they meet it. And that's what building a business comes down to; entrepreneurs see the needs people have, and they find a way to meet them. That is the basis of all entrepreneurship. Remember this as you determine your first product. If you see a need, meet it. A problem solved is a win for the customer; getting paid is a win for you.

4: Your product builds momentum.

I won't say your first dollar is the hardest one to make, but it's close. Once you sell your first ebook, song, poem, glass of wine, bottle of beer, you begin to see the possibilities. Things become real.

Think about it this way - you can't sell your second product until you sell the first one. You can't make your 100th dollar until you've made your first ten.

Building a business, whether it's online or on 5th Avenue, can be tough. When you're first starting, you need quick wins. You need to prove to yourself (and your family) that achieving your dreams is possible. Think about how much pressure nightclubs owners put on the grand opening. They want the hype and the buzz to build and build to the point where it reaches a critical mass that explodes into piles of cash as the people flood in through the doors after waiting in line for hours.

While you can't make a living with a single $10 product, you can if you have ten. It's a proven fact that if your customers buy your first product, they're more likely to buy the second. If it's good of course.

Your existing customers will be your best source of revenue for your next products. Today's customer is tomorrow's repeat buyer. Sales will show you're a winner, and everyone wants to be around a winner. Quick sales and quick wins build quick momentum. And momentum is incredibly powerful!

Establishing Your Expertise

Expertise comes from doing one thing over and over again over an extended period of time. The best athletes, actors, artists and even entrepreneurs become experts by mastering their craft over a period of weeks, months, and years.

First, we want to hire experts. If given a choice, most people would hire the expert instead of the person who merely dabbles. We want to learn from and employ the best if we're going to get the best results or learn to become the best ourselves.

Second, if you want to convince or encourage someone to take action, the only way you'll be able to do it is by having influence over them. Your audience wants to have faith that you know what you're talking about and that the information or services you provide will get them what they need. So, expertise and influence are critical to the success of your business.

My Path to Expertise

For as long as I can remember, I've been curious about how things worked and why people did what they did. Sitting in Introduction to Business during my freshman year at Baylor, I realized I was more interested in *why* people were doing what they were doing and less interested in *what* they were doing. It was then that I decided to change majors and start studying psychology.

At almost every job I've had, managers and trainers have told me I ask too many questions. I never took what I was told and accepted it at face value just because someone claimed it was true. If I am going to sell a product or service, I want to know why it is the best fit for my customers.

My thirst for information has led to some ridicule and a fair amount of teasing from my peers, but my questions are also what have enabled me to be successful. I'm always studying, learning, and trying to understand how things work. If you want people to see you as a knowledgeable resource or an expert, you must ask questions.

I realize not everyone is born with the natural curiosity that caused me to take a watch apart just to peek inside. And that's ok. However, for you to build your business and have influence over your customers, you will need to establish some degree of expertise.

Your influence, like your reputation, is built over time. You can build it, borrow it, or both. Don't worry if other people don't immediately see you as the rockstar you know you are.

Give people time to see the value you offer, and if they don't discover it fast enough, show them. Seek out high-value or high-influence people and give them samples of your product. Ask for feedback, referrals, and testimonials. Don't be afraid to work for free or to give value first. Do what's necessary to stand out and make a difference. Build your influence and you will be successful in business.

23: WEEK SEVEN - DATA DUMP

The world is being reshaped by the convergence of social, mobile, cloud, big data, community, and other powerful forces. The combination of these technologies unlocks an incredible opportunity to connect everything together in a new way and is dramatically transforming the way we live and work.

- Marc Benioff

Over the past several weeks, behind the scenes, you've been collecting data. If you created an Analytics account with Google, a pixel for Facebook, and pasted all the right code into all the right places during Week 1, you now have a wealth of information that's ready to be put to good use.

This week is when we'll finally take a look at that data. You'll learn what you can do with it and how to use the captured information to your advantage. We'll go "outside" again like we did in Week 5 and publish another guest post. And finally, we'll put everything together with two of my favorite tools so you can turn your site into a revenue-generating business.

Step 1: The Tesseract

Inside the fictional world created by Marvel Comics, the Tesseract is the key to unlimited power. Though it's not the power itself, it is the item that opens the door.

In the world of websites and information, your Google Analytics (GA) account is the tesseract that unlocks the power of big data. It is the most powerful, most common and almost always the default option for tracking what happens on and around your website. GA is the key used to unlock an unlimited amount of information about your online presence.

GA's tracking code not only records how people *arrive* on your site but what visitors do while *on* your site as well. While GA is an incredibly powerful tool, I only recommend you use a tiny part of it in the beginning.

Audience Overview

After logging into your GA account, your main dashboard view will be the area found under the Audience tab on the left. If there's not a list of options under "Audience," click the word and you should find where to go next.

The first page inside your dashboard you should look at is the Overview tab under Audience. On this page you'll find:

- **Users** - the number of unique visitors to your site

- **Avg Session Duration** - how long visitors stay on your site

- **Pages / Session** - the number of pages each person looks at while browsing

- **Bounce Rate** - the percentage of visitors who look only at a single page before leaving

- **% New Sessions** - the percentage of visitors who are visiting your site for the very first time

and other valuable information about the people who land on your site. Armed with this information, you know how many people are viewing your content, how long they're staying, and whether your traffic is increasing (or decreasing) over a given window of time. Congratulations! You now know more about your business than most small business owners throughout the history of time.

In business, you may hear the term "up and to the right." Meaning that if your revenue were to be plotted on a line graph, a line that went up and to the right would indicate positive growth over time. When it comes to your GA stats, here's what you'll want to look out for:

- **Users** - you want this to increase over time

- **Average Session Duration** - maintain or increase over time

- **Pages per Session** - maintain or increase over time

- **Bounce Rate** - maintain or decrease over time

- **New Session Percentage** - you want this to stay at or above 50% over time

Acquisition Overview

Now that you know what your visitors are doing once they find your site and take a look around, let's figure out where those visitors are coming from.

On the left side of your page, find the section titled "Acquisition" with two arrows next to it. Under that heading, you'll find the Overview area, and that's where we want to head next.

While we won't spend much time here, there are few key things about which you should be aware. Take a look at the Organic Search and Social channels. If you have ever wondered what percentage of your traffic finds you through an internet search, which is an indication of how good you are at SEO, you'll find that here. If you've ever wondered if your efforts on social media were paying off, you now have your answer.

To give you an idea of the amount of information you can draw from this page, let me share with you some of my numbers.

Over the last twelve months:

- 68.5% of my traffic has come from people using a search engine and finding a relevant link to my site. This tells me I've done a good job with SEO.

- 17.9% has been direct traffic. This is when a visitor types my URL into their browser and hits enter. I can assume people are seeing short links on images or videos and typing them in to get more information. Or, they're going to my home page and then somewhere else on my site.

- 8.6% of my visitors have come from social media outlets. They've clicked a link someone shared on Facebook, Twitter, Instagram, etc.

- 3.9% of my traffic comes from referral sites. These are visitors who find my posts on Lifehack, The Good Men Project, or other site's where I've been published, and click a link back to my site.

The key is to have a mix of referral sources. If you depended entirely on social media, and then Facebook or Twitter decided to change their rules, your traffic numbers would suffer. The same goes for depending too much on search traffic or email marketing.

Variety is the spice of life and diversification is the key to a traffic portfolio that can weather any storm caused by an algorithm change.

Traffic via Search Queries

Also under the Acquisition tab, you'll find a section called "Search Engine Optimization." Under that, you'll see the subheadings of

Queries, Landing Pages, and Geographical Summary. We want to look at the Queries tab. Here we'll find all of the terms people typed into Google to find your site. Is it what you thought it would be?

If you owned wine store, you should see terms related to different types of grapes. You might see words relating to alcohol content, health information, or hours for your location.

These search queries are not only a good indication of how people find you, but they'll also tell you what your customers are thinking about. If you take these search terms and sprinkle them throughout your page, Google, and other search engines will begin to notice that you talk about the same things their users are searching for, and they'll start sending you more traffic.

Lastly, if you find a query labeled "not set," "not provided," "organic," or some other vague term, don't worry, you're not alone. Starting in 2013, Google began hiding that information from us lowly humans. While some of your Adwords paid traffic will unlock some of this data, much of it is still hidden behind Google's veil of secrecy[23]. However, if you combine all of these tools together, you should be able to get a pretty good idea of who is visiting your site, where they're coming from, and what they're looking at while they're there.

Social Traffic

The fourth important view is the Overview area under Social. This can be found inside the Acquisition subheading, and here you'll find the social networks that send you the most traffic.

---

[23] If you want more information about ways to unlock some of that hidden data, you can check out this post from Kissetrics - https://blog.kissmetrics.com/unlock-keyword-not-provided.

For example, I can see that 59% of my social traffic comes from Facebook, 29% comes from Twitter, and the next popular is LinkedIn at 5%.

If I wanted to know where to spend my advertising money, or where I should go to interact with my audience, this Social Overview tells me exactly where I should invest my time and money. Either I boost my existing presence on Facebook, or I can try to increase my reach on LinkedIn.

Since every other network drives less than 1% of my social media referral traffic, I know that either I don't have an audience there, or, if I do, no one is interested enough to click on what's being shared.

Instead of trying to get your existing audience to follow you over to a new network, my suggestion is to connect with them where they already are. If they're on a social platform you don't like, either dig in and learn it anyway or try to build your audience on the social network of your choice.

Popular Pages and Posts

The final Google Analytics view on which you'll want to focus is found under the Behavior main heading and the Site Content subheading. If you click on the section titled "All Pages," you'll find a list of the most popular posts and pages on your site, what percentage of your visitors view them, and other powerful information you can use as your business grows.

Your most popular pages can also be your most profitable. By putting a call to action on the pages your visitors view the most, you can capture the "low hanging fruit" of people visiting your site. You already know what they're looking at so you can make a custom offer just for them.

Since this list also includes blog posts, you know which pieces of content are the most visited and most viewed. They may not be *your* favorite, but they're drawing a lot of eyeballs to your website.

In my case, my second most popular post is one I wrote in a rush one Sunday night at 11:30 pm. The posts you think might connect with your prospects the best might not be the ones they enjoy viewing. This page will tell you what's working.

Also in the "All Pages" view, you'll find the time spent on each of your most popular pages, the bounce rate for each, and the percent of traffic each page contributes to your overall site. For example, by looking at the column labeled "Entrances," I know that my most popular blog post accounts for almost 18% of the traffic for my entire site!

While it would be easy to get overwhelmed with the amount of data inside your GA dashboard, these five dashboard views should give you more than enough information about your website and visitors to plan out where you should spend your time, money and resources.

Step 2: Pixel Perfect

The second most powerful source for online data is the Facebook conversion pixel. While Google Analytics can tell you all about the traffic that comes to your site, Facebook keeps that information locked away. Where Google shows you information about your audience and how they arrived on your site, Facebook allows you to stay in front of your audience after they've left.

Though I won't go into all of the ins-and-outs of Facebook advertising, partly because they're constantly evolving and partly because there's way more than five key "views," I will show you some of the powerful basics.

The Power of the Pixel

Facebook pixels are a digital tag that people receive when they visit a particular page on the internet. When your browser downloads the page, if the Facebook pixel has been added to the code for that page, your browser will also download the pixel of tracking information. Download the pixel and you get tagged. Get tagged and you become part of a custom audience.

The beauty of the pixel is twofold.

First, you're able to determine what pages visitors view on your site and change your marketing in response. For example, if a visitor to your site has the pixel for your sales page but not the pixel for your purchase receipt page, you know they didn't complete a purchase. Armed with the information that they browsed but didn't buy, you can advertise for your products in their Facebook newsfeed or promote a video that shows off the features of your product or service.

Second, the Facebook pixel allows you to promote directly to a "warm" audience who already knows who you are. Because you can promote posts or create ads that target people tagged by a particular pixel, you can make sure your ad for colorful socks is shown only to people who've visited your sales page for colorful socks.

The power of the pixel lies in the specificity it provides. Instead of putting an ad in front of anyone who's interested in a given topic, you can aim your ad to interested people who are already aware that you're a provider. Facebook pixels enable you to target your audience even after they've left your website, and that's a powerful thing!

Custom Audiences

Also within your Facebook ads manager is the ability to create custom audiences. These audiences can be comprised of people who have all been tagged with the same pixel, but there's another way you can use them to great effect. By uploading your existing email list, you can create a custom audience of people who have already opted-in to receive your email marketing messages. Talk about staying in front of your audience!

Though the exact steps to do this will differ between email services and the current method used by Facebook, here are the necessary steps to create this custom audience:

1. Log into your email marketing service.

2. Navigate to your list of contacts.

3. Export your entire list of contacts, from all lists to a comma separated value, or CSV file (Note: you can even include people who unsubscribe on your export list. Since you're not emailing them, you're not breaking any rules).

4. Open the exported CSV file and delete all fields except for the column with the email lists. Also, delete the first row that includes the heading.

5. Save the new file full of email addresses.

6. Log into your Facebook ad manager account.

7. Create a new custom audience (usually found under Tools and Audiences).

8. Choose "Customer List" from the pop-up window.

9. Upload you new file or copy and paste your list of email addresses.

And that's it! After a few minutes, Facebook will compare your list of email addresses with user accounts and add the matches to your new custom audience. Now, when you choose to promote content or create a new ad for your next product, you can decide to market to people you already have information for.

This level of retargeting or remarketing is part of the reason why Gary Vaynerchuck and I are such a fans of Facebook advertising. Hopefully, you're beginning to see the power of the pixel too!

Use the custom audience capabilities to get your posts, videos and content in front of your audience even after they've left your website. Promote book launches, special events, new blog posts and other things that add value to your audience.

Step 3: Guest Posting

In Week 5 of the Roadmap, we talked in detail about the value of the guest appearance. While that discussion primarily surrounded joint ventures, partnerships, and co-hosting events, this section is focused on guest posting on other websites. Again, if blogging isn't your thing, you can substitute in the type of content that best fits your brand.

Guest posting allows you to get your message in front of a new audience. Sites like Entrepreneur.com, MindBodyGreen.com, GoodMenProject.com, Lifehack.org, and others are always on the lookout for great content written by fantastic writers. Most of the time, you just have to ask or apply, and you will have the opportunity to submit your proposal to an editor for publishing.

Whether you're submitting a guest post proposal to one of these major publications or to one of your fellow content creator's sites, keep in mind who *their* audience is, not *your* audience. The best proposals are the ones that offer to provide value to the readers, viewers and listeners of your future host. Tailor your content to match the medium and you'll be much more likely to get the opportunity to share your message.

Your homework for this week is to pick three sites and write or record a piece of content you can submit. Some sites want the entire piece, others just want an outline, so do your research. And, if they don't accept your guest post, you can always post it on your site instead.

Guest posting has been one of the best tools I've used for growing my audience. From posts published on smaller sites when

I first got started, to articles written for major publications like Lifehack and The Good Men Project, I've always been an advocate for guest posting. And, I've seen some great results, and I know you will too.

Step 4: Turning a Profit

Most businesses aren't profitable for quite a while after they first open their doors. If you took out a $100,000 loan to rent office space, build or buy inventory, pay utilities and all of the other things that go along with opening a storefront, it could take years to pay off your loan.

Keeping my business in the black is something I've thought about from the very beginning. In fact, in the early days, my blog was just a hobby; I didn't want to spend my play money on anything to do with my website. As I mentioned before, I used free themes and free tools for years before finally deciding to upgrade to paid versions or premium software.

One of the beauties of having an online business is that the startup costs can be quite low. Another one of those beautiful things is that there are tools we can use that either are free, or they're pay-as-you-go.

In step four, we're going to look at two of the tools I have used for several years to accept payments and deliver digital products. Then we'll wrap up Week 7 with some of the tactics you can use to help get your products in front of as many new customers as possible.

Creating Your Store

The first tool I want you to look at is a free plugin for WordPress called Easy Digital Downloads (EDD). You can download this free plugin for WordPress and find all of the upgrade options at

EasyDigitalDownloads.com. If you plan to primarily sell digital goods, i.e., anything you don't have to package and ship, EDD is what I would recommend.

If you plan on selling something where you need to capture a billing and shipping address, or if you'd need to calculate shipping charges, EDD is more than capable of handling the job, but you may want to take a look at the WooCommerce theme and plugin found at www.woothemes.com/woocommerce.

Both tools use the freemium model I mentioned in Chapter 13. Each plugin is free to use, but some of the nicer features are paid. Again, this isn't a bait and switch. Think of the freemium model as an a la carte menu - we only have to pay for what we know we'll use.

Both WooCommerce and EDD come as either a WordPress theme and plugin combo, or they can be used as standalone plugins with your existing theme. Since EDD is the tool I use and recommend, that's what we'll talk about here. However, if you'd rather use WooCommerce, you'll still get a lot of value out of the next section because the principles are mostly universal and can apply to any tool you choose to use for your online store.

Like any store owner, you'll want to create multiple products and test different layouts to see how things look in your browser. Instead of putting cans or boxes of cereal on your shelves, you'll be playing with titles, subtitles, product descriptions and columns.

It's not as complicated as it sounds, trust me. Anything I've done, you can do too, and if I can figure out how to use all of this software, you can too. But I assure you, it's easier than you think. The plugins will do most of the heavy lifting for you.

The first thing you'll need to do, after deciding which plugin and theme combo you want to use, is to install it. Like any plugin, you'll be able to upload it from your WordPress Dashboard under the Plugins menu. Click on "Add New" and either search for the plugin from the directory or upload it from your computer if you downloaded it.

Next, activate the plugin. WooCommerce has a few more steps, but it's an easy enough process to follow. Both plugins have the ability to automatically create and publish pages for your checkout, purchase success, confirmation and any other pages you might need. Check your list of pages after activating the plugin and if you don't see the new pages listed there, go into the plugin's settings and click the "Generate" button.

Third, navigate to the "Payment Gateways" section of the plugin's menu. This will be where you'll add your PayPal email address to connect your account to your store. The money from anything you sell on your site will be automatically transferred to your PayPal account.

A free e-commerce plugin you can use to sell your stuff, and a free PayPal account to accept payments from customers around the world? I told you this would be cool! Using the tools and method I just outlined, you will only pay a fee when you make money. PayPal charges nothing unless you sell a product or service, and even then it's less than 3% of the amount you make.

Finally, you need to create and design your first product. Before you talk yourself out of it and anxiety sets in, stop worrying about it. Your first product won't make you rich, and it won't ruin your business if it fails. If you hit it out of the park with your first product, you'd not only be the first person in history, but you'd have nowhere to go afterward but downhill.

Whether it's a widget, a piece of software, a special recipe passed down from your grandmother, or an ebook, the creation of your inaugural product is a pivotal moment in the launch of your new business.

Your first product, whether it's $10 or $100:

- Tells the world who you are, what your business is about, and what types of amazing things we can expect from you in the future. It sets the stage.

- Provides an accessible entry point to your company and immerses your clients in your culture. My suggestion is to create your product or service in such a way that you don't have to charge more than $100 for it. At $100, your product isn't so expensive that it would be a turn-off to prospects who don't yet know you.

- Gives you the opportunity to provide a substantial amount of value for an insubstantial sum of money. When you launch your business with a product that blows people away, you've set the tone for what's to come down the road.

I don't want you to get overly stressed about developing the first item you'll put up for sale. But, I do want you to put your very best work into it. First impressions are powerful, and you want your customers to keep coming back long after they've enjoyed what you offered.

Making a Sale

If you can't accept payment, you can't make a sale. Sure, you can barter services for products, and vice versa, but you won't be able to barter your way to $10,000 a month in revenue. To start, build and grow your business, you will need a way to accept currency in exchange for your product or service.

When I began, I used PayPal exclusively. Their free plan will allow you to integrate their payment processor with e-commerce tools like Easy Digital Downloads, WooCommerce, and other design tools. Because of the added security and customization options, I switched to Stripe late in 2014, but I still use PayPal for several things, and I recommend you start there as well.

Tips for Making Your First Sale

- **Visibility** - If your visitors don't know you have something for sale, they can't buy it. You can use your site's sidebar to highlight new and best-selling products. You should also include a link to your products or store page on your menu and emails.

- **Security** - If you're planning to do a lot of transactions on your site, consider upgrading your hosting service to include an SSL certificate. SSLs and their accompanying badges will help buyers feel safe and confident about purchasing from you.

- **Simplicity** - Make it easy for prospective buyers to purchase your products. Eliminate unnecessary clicks between your product's sales page and your checkout. If you don't require a customer's address or phone number, don't ask for it. Make your buying process as streamlined as possible.

- **Scannable** - Make your sales pages easy to scan. Like walking through a clothing store and browsing for the perfect outfit, your customers should be able to scan your page and quickly decide if your product is right for them. Using the following tools will help you make your sales page scannable.

  o **Headlines** - Use big, bold headlines to attract the attention of your prospective buyers. Use powerful language to pull them in, catch their interest, and entice them to scroll down and scan your page.

  o **Bullets** - When you're writing the sales copy, bullets are great tools to highlight features and benefits. Features are the details; benefits are what your customer will be able to do with them. For example, a 61" 1080p TV (features) will allow everyone to make the most out of family movie night (benefits). Focus on what your product allows your buyers to do. An easy way to do this is to insert the phrase "so that" after your product's details and fill in the blank. For example, "This new 61" 1080p has the clearest picture imaginable *so that* you can see all of your movies just like you were in the theater."

- **Social Proof** - Getting your first sale is often one of the most difficult things to do. Nobody wants to be the guinea pig. To overcome people's fears of being a crash test dummy, use social proof in the form of testimonials, product reviews, case studies, before-and-after photos, etc.

- **Guarantees** - Calm your customers' fears about making a purchase by offering a thirty, sixty or ninety-day satisfaction guarantee. Very few people will ask for a return, and even fewer will abuse their ability to do so. However, you'll calm their fears by making the offer in the first place. In my short time of doing business, I've had to give less than five returns or exchanges.

One of the best resources on copywriting is Ray Edwards' book, *Writing Riches*. As Ray says, copywriting is "simply salesmanship in print." If you want to build a business, you're going to have to sell something. And, to increase your sales, you must improve your skills.

To recap Week 7, you now have a mountain of data and products to sell. By reviewing Google Analytics, you know how people are finding your site and what they're looking at while they browse. Facebook's pixels allow you to virtually "tag" your visitors so you can market to them after they've left your site. Each guest post you write puts your message and brand in front of a new and ever-growing audience. And PayPal and Easy Digital Downloads allow you to sell products and only pay fees when you make money. What a busy week!

If you've done everything we've talked about in the Roadmap, you should have a pretty good understanding of how business can be done online. By providing value first, building a following of people interested in what you're doing, and offering a quality solution to a particular set of problems, anyone can build a business. Entrepreneurs see the needs people have, then they provide a solution. That, in a nutshell, is the basis of entrepreneurship.

24: WEEK EIGHT - MARKETING AND PROMOTION

People don't buy what you do; they buy why you do it.
- Simon Sinek

B efore I started my own business, I wasn't a huge fan of marketing. I looked at the people in the marketing department, and most of the work they did, as superfluous. The way I saw it, a good salesperson did their own marketing, but the people who claimed to be marketers had no business selling anything to anyone.

Though I'm not quite sure my opinions have changed, at least not regarding corporate redundancy and extraneous spending, I now see the incredible power of marketing. A successful entrepreneur is always marketing and always selling. While I don't advocate you resort to shoving your products down the throats of uninterested people, I do encourage you to be on the lookout for new opportunities to build your business and new problems you to solve.

Over the past several weeks, you've formed your business idea, built your foundation and put the pieces together, and last week you set everything up to start making money. Now it's time to tell the world what you're about, share why you're so passionate about it, and explain how you're going eliminate their pain. Now we talk about marketing and promotion.

But, before we dive directly into marketing, let me share with you one of the most valuable business concepts I can share with you. When I mentioned this to my corporate colleagues, the idea I'm about to share with you either went over their heads or they didn't care about it all. However, it will be one of the keys to the success of your business.

Mindshare

Most business people are familiar with a term "market share," but it's rare I come across someone forward-thinking enough to think about what I like to call, "mindshare."

In case you're unfamiliar with market share, let me explain. If you have $10, and you choose to spend three of them at Walmart, then Walmart has a 30% market share. Using the same analogy on a larger scale, if there are a million people and 300,000 of them regularly get their products from Walmart, then Walmart has a 30% share of the local market.

While this math is fine for some companies, it shouldn't be fine for you. Yes, having thirty cents of every dollar spent with your business would be nice, but that's not what we're going for. Yet.

If you want to build a business and think like a savvy entrepreneur, think about mindshare instead of market share.

What is mindshare?

Great question.

Mindshare is the percentage of time your clients and prospective clients spend thinking about you or your business as a means of alleviating their pain or meeting their needs. For example, where electronics are concerned, Best Buy has almost a 100%

mindshare for my household. Whenever we need something electronic, nearly 100% of the time, we think about going to Best Buy to get it. It doesn't matter if they have the product or not, there's a good chance I'm going to bestbuy.com to at least see if they offer it.

Other examples of high mindshare could be your family doctor who you'd never leave and always call first for advice. Another example could be the reliable mechanic who has never let you down and has always been able to fix your vehicles. You simply wouldn't trust anyone else. Even if your doctor and mechanic can't fix your issue, they know who can, and are able to make a reliable referral.

When you can get to that point in your business, where you've inserted yourself into the very fabric of the lives of your clients, you've won.

Think achieving mindshare is impossible? It's not.

Earning mindshare is done one client at a time. It's achieved by offering the best information possible, even if that information doesn't lead to a sale, or, that information leads to a sale for someone else.

When you become a trusted advisor to your customers and clients, they'll come to you first, even if they aren't sure if you can help them. Establishing a reputation as a trusted advisor was one of the strategies that contributed to my incredible success during my time at Dell. My customers knew I'd give them an honest answer every time, even if it didn't help me. If you treat your customers the same way, you'll earn their mindshare, and they'll keep coming to you as their source for information.

As you begin to plan how you're going to market your business, always keep in mind how you can increase your mindshare with your customers. If you sell cars, share information relevant to the types of tires, windshield wipers, or motor oil your clients may need. If you sell sports equipment, consider reviewing popular local or travel destinations your customers could visit and use the gear they bought from you.

Build a network of partners you can rely on when your clients come to you for trustworthy information. Ask yourself, "What else will they need?" and begin building your extended team to help you answer the question.

Trust me; this works!

Step 1: Social Media Marketing

I remember when my blog only received about 125 visitors each month. I knew my content was fairly good, but I couldn't figure out why no one was coming to read it.

When you first start your business, one of the biggest challenges you'll face is overcoming obscurity. No one knows who you are, and that's a problem. You could have the sweetest treats, the speediest software, or the most expert advice, but if your potential clients don't know you exist, they can't hire you.

Social media marketing is an excellent way to spread the word and raise awareness about your business. If you're using the tactics I shared in Week 4, and you're creating valuable content for your audience, you should be using social media to market your business. Every blog post, video, infographic, podcast episode or interview you produce is something you should share via social media.

You can create fifteen-second teaser videos for Instagram and link to the full video in your bio. You could share a link on Twitter that takes people back to the video you uploaded to your Facebook group or page. Use one network to "cross-pollinate" to your audiences on other platforms. Give value fast and share that value publicly on social media.

But, if you're only sharing your information once, you're going to miss 99.9% of your audience.

Let me show you what I mean.

Imagine that your bakery had the recipe for the best blackberry cobbler within 100 miles. Every day, just as your cobblers came out of the oven, you turned on your OPEN sign, stepped out on your front stoop and yelled, "The world's greatest cobbler, as voted by you the community, is now hot, fresh and ready!" Afterward, you went back inside to wait for the inevitable flood of traffic to come bursting through the door, money in hand, waiting to buy your cobbler.

How long do you think your company would last?

Anyone who didn't happen to be within earshot when you made the morning announcement would have missed the message. That means, if they weren't in the right place at the right time, they'd never know they were so close to the best cobbler in the world. It doesn't matter if the dessert was voted the best and there was plenty of social proof and testimonials to back it up; if they aren't aware, they can't buy. And, just because the cobblers don't sell that day, doesn't mean your dessert is bad or that people hate what you're making.

Are you doing the same thing in your business?

Social media is one of the best tools we have as entrepreneurs to help us step out from the shadows and overcome obscurity. The very nature of social media encourages "virality" through sharing. But, if we miss your message we can't share it, like it, heart it, retweet it, or interact with it in any way.

If you're only sharing your content once, you're like the baker who only announces his fresh pies once. Your readers, subscribers, listeners, viewers and fans might not be where they can see or hear your message when you deliver it. And, if they are, they may not be in a position to anything about it. By sharing your message and the value it brings more than once, you can more effectively capture the attention of the people who need to hear it.

Now let's look at strategies to keep in mind when you share.

Lifetime of a Tweet

Twitter moves fast. Some reports say the life of a tweet, the amount of time each short message has to be seen, is less than twenty seconds. Other reports say it's almost twenty minutes.[24]

Regardless of your tweet's longevity, the lesson is that if you want your tweet to be seen, you should share it more than once. Social media tools like Buffer and Hootsuite make repeated sharing easy.

Twitter (and almost every social feed) moves too fast for you to share once and be done. The same truth applies to other networks as well, so share when your audience is going to see it.

Reach of Facebook

Getting a post on Facebook seen in the newsfeed of a significant percentage of your audience used to be free. And easy.

Now, unless you spend money to reach a higher portion of your audience, the average reach of a post shared on your Facebook page is less than 5%. Even though Facebook is an incredibly powerful social tool, that power comes at a price.

However, it doesn't have to cost an arm and a leg to promote your content. You can boost a post for as little as $5. Don't do what I did and avoid spending the five bucks as your way of fighting the system. Boost your content to the most engaged members of your audience and everyone wins.

---

[24] https://www.quora.com/what-is-the-lifespan-of-a-tweet

Share Multiple Times a Day

Let me ask you a question. When it's 7:00 in the morning in New York and everyone is sipping their lattes and browsing their favorite blogs, what are the people in California doing?

They're sleeping. That's what they're doing.

If you share a link to your blog, video or a new piece of content at 6:45 in the morning so it's fresh for your readers on the east coast, you also just shared it at 3:45 am for the millions of people in California, Oregon, and Washington. While an early morning post in the United States may be perfect for an after lunch read for everyone in the England, it's in the middle of the night in Australia.

An online business is a global business so share your valuable message multiple times a day.

Share Across Multiple Platforms

At the time of this publication, there's no search function within the Snapchat social media platform. The only way to get new followers is for them to see you sharing about your "snaps" on other platforms and then look you up in Snapchat. The same goes for finding people you want to follow. Since usernames can contain numbers and characters in addition to letters, you'd have to see my post on Facebook or Twitter before learning how to find me on Snapchat. Even after spending a few weeks directing my followers over to my stories on Snapchat, a large percentage of my audience never saw what I was sharing.

If I only shared my material on Snapchat, most of my audience wouldn't see it. The same principle applies to every social platform out there. If you only share your videos on Facebook, the people in your audience who prefer Twitter, Pinterest, LinkedIn or any other platform wouldn't see it. To share your message, you must share it across multiple communities.

Your task for Step 1 is to create short, sharable teasers for every piece of content you create. I keep mine in an Excel spreadsheet; you can do the same or use Google Sheets for free. I also create three to five different teasers for every post I write so I don't share the same blurb over and over again.

Then, create a free account with Buffer, Hootsuite or the sharer of your choice, then begin adding these teasers to your schedule. Be sure you mix up the order so you don't share the same post back to back, and don't forget to include your older evergreen content as well.

Step 2: Marketing to Find Clients

As I mentioned before, getting your first client can be difficult. Few people want to be early adopters, and even fewer will want to be your test dummy.

However, once you start getting positive reviews, be sure you share them. Sometimes that means on your products page, sometimes it means at the front of your book, and sometimes that means on social media. Sharing positive reviews, specifically a before and after transformation, is an effective way to attract new clients.

Another tip is to market the end result. If someone loses twenty pounds after following your program, share that. If a business saves ten percent by switching to your service, share that. Even if the transformation is something as intangible as going from being miserable and tired to happy and alert, well, of course, you should share that!

If your blog posts, videos, recipes, or other content is making someone's life better, and it should, you already have a powerful marketing message.

Lastly, if you have a piece of work you know will benefit someone specific, be sure you reach out to them and ask them to read or watch it. If you have a program that will make their life easier or better, don't hide it, share it. And, ask for feedback afterward. This feedback could help guide you when you develop your next product and may even turn into a valuable testimonial.

Step 3: Email Marketing

If you were going to sign up for a new account on Facebook, in addition to your first and last names, what information would you be asked to provide?

Your email address.

And your birthday.

What about when creating a new account with Twitter, LinkedIn, Snapchat, Pinterest, or even Amazon and iTunes?

Your email address.

While, yes, technically you can use your cell phone number to create your Facebook account, and yes, you can log into Pinterest with your Facebook profile, I have yet to find a reliable statistic showing how many people actually do that. Not only is email a practical requirement for our online and social lives, but it's also a key component of communication in our offline and daily life. And it has been for at least the last twenty years.

Email is one of the best tools you have at your disposal for marketing your business. Even social media gurus and Facebook Ad experts like Amy Porterfield[25] and Rick Mulready,[26] still capture email addresses on their sites and on their checkout pages. While social media sites and the advertising options they provide are valuable, they're largely extensions or add-ons to your email efforts.

---

[25] Find more at http://www.amyporterfield.com/

[26] Find more at http://rickmulready.com/

As you're now eight weeks into your new business, it's time to take a serious look at how you can use email to market your products, services, and brand. We'll learn more about using email and how to "indoctrinate" your subscribers in Chapter 28, but for now, let's take a brief look at how you can begin using email now.

Purpose

Every email should have a purpose. Before writing your subject line, ask yourself two questions. First, ask, "Why am I writing this?" Second, ask, "Why would someone want to read this?"

If you establish a trend of sending valuable emails your subscribers want to read, those subscribers will be more likely to read your emails down the road. The reverse is true as well; send emails that waste people's time and they'll stop opening them.

Sometimes the purpose of your emails is to inform, other times it's to entertain. Sharing your story, the behind-the-scenes look at your business, is a great reason to email your subscribers, especially in the beginning.

Call to Action

Gmail and other email services gauge the value of an email based on the actions the receivers take. Do they delete them immediately? Do they click the links inside? Do they archive the emails and go back to them later?

By including a call to action, like "click to read more," "reply with your answer," "buy now," etc., you're not only driving engagement, but your subscribers are proving to their provider that your emails are appreciated.

Frequency

Have you ever gotten an email from someone but couldn't remember who they were or how you knew them? Email your list often enough that they don't forget who you are, but not too often that you annoy them.

In the early days, email them more often. As time goes on and after a positive relationship is established, you can reduce your frequency. I email new subscribers three to four times in the first week while the relationship is new and exciting. Then I reduce the frequency to one email approximately every ten days.

Unsubscribe

If you're emailing as part of your business, as opposed to emailing your friends about lunch, you must include a link to allow recipients to unsubscribe. It's the law.

That means you can't use Gmail or a mail merge to email your subscribers in bulk. Use a free email marketing service like MailChimp or Benchmark to send your emails. Services like these keep you compliant.

Spam

Inboxes are getting smarter every day. Sometimes they're too smart for their own good.

Use tools like Mail-Tester.com to test the "spammy-ness" of your email before you send it. Copy the contents of your newsletter or email into a new message, send it to the address provided by Mail Tester, and you'll get a grade. Some of the information provided about your message's content will be technical, but a large portion will be things you should fix before sending it out to your list. I run 100% of my email messages through this tool and others like it before sending them to my audience.

Autoresponders

Premium email service providers like ActiveCampaign allow you to create autoresponders and automations that will automatically send emails based on predetermined conditions. For example, you can send a new subscriber an email after they've been on your list for five minutes, then again after two days, and again after a week.

Autoresponders are a great way to create touch points over an extended period of time. If your emails are evergreen, or timeless, you can send them to your new subscribers over many months or even years and provide them with value over time.

For your efforts with email marketing, use autoresponders to share relevant information with your subscribers with a call to action to learn more, make a purchase, or respond to questions. Each email should have a clearly defined purpose

Give, Give, Give, Ask

No one wants to be sold to every time they open their inbox. Provide value to your subscribers first, and second, and third, and then ask for their business. Rinse and repeat.

To follow this formula, I moved my community survey to later in my autoresponder series. Even though I don't ask for a sale, I ask for time. I first offer a free resource, followed by a bit of my story. Then I tell new subscribers why I believe in them and what they can expect from me. Finally, I ask them to tell me more about who they are through my survey.

***

As I mentioned at the beginning of Part III, I almost didn't include this Roadmap in the book. It wasn't until I stepped back and examined what I had that I realized what was missing. And what an oversight that would have been!

From the very beginning, my goal with this book has been to outline what I would do if I had to start all over. I wanted to share what I did well, and why, what I didn't do so well, and what I learned. By including the Roadmap, I laid the groundwork for anyone who wants to be successful in business. Whether you're a blogger, a speaker, or the Army veteran opening the donut shop down the road, I believe this path forward is a great one.

Now that you've poured the foundation, and the concrete is beginning to set, it's time to grab an energy drink and start putting the pieces together in a way that will make you money.

PART IV - WHO NEEDS AN ENERGY DRINK?

You may encounter many defeats, but you must not be defeated. In fact, it may be necessary to encounter the defeats, so you can know who you are, what you can rise from, how you can still come out of it."
- Maya Angelou

At this point you might be feeling a bit tired, maybe exhausted, and like you could use a coffee. It's ok; this is a lot to take in. What you've been reading took me years to learn, months to implement, and days to put into words on paper. You've taken it all in over a matter of weeks.

However, this is not the time to slow down, take a break or rest.

Most people quit before they build any momentum. Most people quit right before they start doing the thing which will get results.

So, pour your favorite energy drink (I prefer a black coffee), grab a fresh pen or highlighter, and keep going. It's time to push through, bet on yourself, and get (back) to work.

25: THE WORST ADVICE EVER

The advice I would give to someone is to not take anyone's advice.
- Eddie Murphy

Back in the early 1990s, when I was about ten years old, McDonald's was giving away movies as part of their Happy Meal promotions. I remember my dad pulling around to place our order and asking me which movie I wanted with my cheeseburger and fries. Against his advice, I chose a dinosaur movie.

What I should have asked for was *Field of Dreams*. If you're not familiar with the film, the story follows a man named Ray and the corn field behind his house. One night, Ray hears a mysterious voice whose message leads Ray to build a baseball diamond in the yard. After building the diamond, the ghosts of famous ball players start showing up to play. The movie's producers, actors, and director do a good job of making ghosts in a corn field not as creepy as the concept sounds.

What the mysterious voice said to Ray was, "If you build it, he will come." And, with that as his motivation, Ray, played by Kevin

Costner, gets to work constructing his baseball diamond so he can have one last chance to play with baseball legends.

While I have no problem with the movie, or even the line, "if you build it he will come," I take issue when people apply that mentality to their website, or business.

Today, people change "he" to "they," and get "If you build it *they* will come," and it's the worst advice you could ever receive about building a business.

Waiting around for something to happen is why many starters never succeed. If you want something to happen, *you* have to *make it happen!*

Just because you have a blog does not mean readers will start reading it. Just because you throw your passion into podcasting doesn't mean anyone will listen to it. The internet is too big, and there are too many websites. You can't sit back and wait to be discovered. It won't happen.

In this internet age, putting up a website and sitting back to wait is like opening up a back-alley storefront, hanging a sign on the door that says "Joe's Place" and hoping people will walk in. Not only would your store be almost impossible to find, but who the heck even knows what "Joe's Place" is? Is it a bar? Is it a pizzeria? Is it an accounting firm?

No. Instead, "Joe's Place" is a bookstore with comfy couches and a quiet place to read, write, and work while sipping cappuccino and creating art. But no one knows because the name wasn't descriptive and the owner didn't tell anyone about it. No flyers, no ad in the paper, nothing.

Think that's a little far-fetched?

I thought you might say that.

If you think "no one would actually do that," then consider how "Joe's Place" is any different from thousands of websites out there named after a person. It isn't. Joe's Place is the same thing as joesplace.com or joesmith.com or ellorywells.com.

Businesses, websites and blogs who open a storefront or a website and sit back to wait are putting their faith in the bad advice of "if you build it, they will come." Entrepreneurs with businesses who do that are just as destined to fail as Joe's Place at the back of the alley hidden behind the dumpster.

Fortunately for us, there's something we can do about it.

26: HOW TO GET MORE TRAFFIC

*For me, the most fun is change or growth. There are
definitely elements of both that I like. Launching a
business is kind of like a motorboat: You can go very
quickly and turn fast.*
- ***Tony Hsieh***

If you were opening a storefront, you'd be concerned with
location. The better the location, the more the foot traffic. The
more people coming in your door, the higher your sales. In your
business, the same strategy will apply. The more people visit your
website, the more money you'll eventually make.

But how do you get traffic to your site? How do you get
eyeballs to read your words, ears to listen to your podcasts and
people to care about what you're doing?

There are five primary types of traffic to your site: search
engines, social media, direct, referral, and email. Let's take a look
at each one of these and why they matter to your business. Then,
we'll look at ways to make each of these traffic sources work for
you and how they'll help you build your business.

Traffic from Search Engines

When it comes to search engines, there are two main players, Google, and Bing. While other search engines have come and gone, none has had the impact on the internet and our culture that Google has had over the past twenty years. Though Google is the largest player, Bing shouldn't be ignored as it is the platform built into all new Windows-based computer systems. Bing also handles the search for popular sites like Yahoo.

These search engines sort through millions of websites every day. Google and Bing collect indexes of websites like the card catalog in a library so they can provide relevant information to searchers. Each company has gone to great lengths to only show the best information to the people using their services. Things like on page SEO (Search Engine Optimization), backlinks, and keyword relevance all play a role in determining which sites are shown to searchers and which sites remain hidden on the dreaded "second page."

Sound complicated?

Let me explain.

SEO used to be a mythical beast slain only by the most technical and internet-savvy. Fortunately for us, it's now much simpler. SEO is little more than a search engine's ability to understand the idea behind each post you publish and page you create. If you Googled my name, for example, you'd most likely see my website, social media pages, and articles I've published on other websites around the internet. SEO is what allows Google and Bing to show relevant and accurate results to their users.

Tools like Yoast SEO,[27] a freemium plugin for WordPress, make it easy for beginners like you and me to make our content searchable. By downloading the plugin and activating it on your site,

---

[27] https://wordpress.org/plugins/wordpress-seo/

you'll get a color-coded guide to improving the "search-ability" grade and SEO ranking of every post you write. Things like how many times a keyword appears on the page (keyword density), the number of relevant links to other sites (outbound links), and appropriately tagged images will go a long way to improving the grade of each page. Get a green light from the plugin and you're ready to publish.

Backlinks are links from other websites back to your site. The best backlinks are from sites similar to yours and whose readers are similar to your readers. Ideally, they're from sites with more authority and a larger audience than yours. Backlinks from irrelevant or spam sites are not beneficial to your site and will hurt your domain's reputation with search engines.

My website receives just over fifty percent of its traffic from search engines. By using tools like Yoast SEO, I've optimized (or gotten the green light) on almost all of my posts and pages, and search engines send me readers every day. SEO is *not* dead, and it can be one of your best assets for getting traffic to your new website.

Social Media Referrals

Over the past decade, social media has exploded. Eighty percent of the population in the United States is on Facebook and most of those people log in every day. Twitter has nearly 300 million users, and LinkedIn is one of the top twenty most popular sites on the internet. Plus, new social media sites pop up all the time, each begging for the attention of its users and offering you a way to connect with your readers, clients and customers. When properly used, social media is a powerful driver of traffic to your site.

Since eighty percent of the population is on Facebook, statistically that means that approximately eighty percent of your potential audience is on there too. Unless your target market is naturalists or the Amish, there's a good chance your ideal client, reader, listener or customer is scrolling through their news feed every single day.

By sharing your new posts, podcast episodes, new products and features to your timeline, you put your message in front of your network. If you make your posts public, whenever your friends like or share your posts, their friends are likely to see your posts as well. That means whenever your mom (who could be your first reader) likes your post what you're doing and how you're changing lives, your mom's friends, coworkers, etc. may also see your posts.

Your reach on Facebook, as on most social networks, is exponential; the more people are engaged, the more people will see your posts. It's like the old pyramid schemes, you tell ten people, they each tell ten people, and soon you have access to 10,000.

LinkedIn, Twitter, Pinterest and the others function mostly in the same way. If one of your Twitter followers retweets your link, image or update, your tweet could be in front of their entire audience. If someone who follows one of your boards on Pinterest re-pins one of your posts, your recipe, blog post, video, etc., will be shown to all of their followers as well.

Social media is an incredible tool if used in the right ways and if you put in the extra effort to make a real and personal connection with the people in your network.

However, social media, as with any platform, has its challenges.

When beginners first have something to share, they're excited yet timid about telling their network about what they've just created. I come across new bloggers every day who are hesitant to share their latest post because they're afraid they'll be seen as a "self-promoter." They don't want to come across as needy, arrogant, or braggadocios.

And that's got to stop. If you're not willing to share your posts and promote your products, you can't expect other people to do it for you. Where social media is concerned, you must share your links more than once.

Think about it this way. If you shared a link to your latest post at 7 am to catch your east coast readers before they head to work, you've just shared it while the millions of people living in California are asleep. The biggest mistake I see new entrepreneurs make is sharing their content only once in fear of sharing too often. Because they don't want to be a called a "shameless self-promoter" they pull back too far and end up not sharing often enough. When you first start, you have to tell everyone about what you're doing.

Consider when you're on social media and when you typically scroll through your news feed. For me, I check Facebook in the morning before I start my day, during lunch, mid-afternoon when things slow down, and then several times in the evening. If you've only shared in the morning, the odds are, your audience won't scroll through hours' worth of updates to find yours.

You can measure the average lifespan of a tweet in seconds; the visibility of a status update on Facebook is just a few minutes. While you shouldn't share the same thing every hour of every day, you should share new content three to four times throughout a twenty-four hour period.

Yes, there are several researched and tested strategies about when and how many times you should share your content via social media.[28] But, it comes down to this, you have to share your content for it to be seen. When I started sharing my own content, my traffic tripled within a few days.

One thing I teach all of my coaching clients is to change the way they think about their content. Instead of being timid or shy about sharing your message, be bold. Think of your potential audience as being dehydrated and thirsty, and what you have to share is the much-needed water they're looking for. If you believe in what you're saying, you owe it to them to share it.

---

[28] https://blog.bufferapp.com/how-often-post-social-media

Imagine that you were a financial blogger, and you just wrote the blog post "10 Stupidly Simple Ways to Squash Your Debt." Here I am, your friend, in way over my head and drowning in bills. After I declare bankruptcy and lose my house I find out you had *exactly* what I needed but you were too afraid to tell me about it. How pissed off at you should I be?

If you stand behind your message and your work, you have an obligation to share it with the people who need it. At least once.

Believe in what you have to say, have the facts to back it up, share your message with the people who would benefit from hearing it, and you'll start building a loyal audience in no time.

A few tips for sharing via social media:

Test different types of posts. Share text only, image only, video only, and see what works. Try longer blurbs versus shorter ones and see which status updates get the most likes, clicks and engagement. Also, test sharing at different times of both day and night. With the algorithm changes in Facebook and Twitter, video content will be more likely to get engagement than plain text, but that could all change by the time this book hits the shelves.

Images also tend to get more views and engagement than text. Try doing short, one to two-minute trailer videos for every podcast episode or blog post. Tease the full content and share the teaser video directly to Facebook and Twitter, and upload it to YouTube. The more places you can get your videos the better.

Use tools like Buffer, HootSuite, TweetDeck, Edgar and others to schedule your shares in the morning and have them release throughout the day. Most of these social media tools will tell you which types of updates get the most interaction and let you use them again at a later time. Combine these tools with the insights from Google Analytics, and you'll have a good idea about which updates get the most engagement and which social networks are driving the most traffic back to your site. Go where your audience is engaging with your content and nurture those relationships.

Direct Traffic

Direct traffic is made up of visitors who have bookmarked your site and click that bookmark every time they want to come back. If the amount of direct traffic increases over time, it's a good indication that the number of loyal readers you have has also increased over time.

For example, if you type www.ellorywells.com into your browser and hit "Enter" that would be direct traffic. If I shared a link on Facebook to my latest blog post and you clicked it, your visit would be considered "social" traffic.

Referral and Email

Together, referral and email traffic account for less than ten percent of my site's traffic. Your numbers could be different, but here's what they are and how to leverage them to grow your audience.

Referral traffic comes from the backlinks we mentioned before. These are often called inbound links. If you write a guest post on another blog, or someone features you on their podcast, and a reader clicks a link in your bio that takes them to your About Page, that's a referral.

By guest posting, leaving value-adding comments, and getting featured on other websites, you'll build a network of backlinks which will increase the amount of referral traffic you receive. If you're interviewed as a guest on a podcast, make sure they link to your site so people can find you and the host can refer their audience to your valuable content.

Email traffic is any traffic that clicks a link in an email and lands on your site. Pretty basic, right?

If you're sending regular emails, often called campaigns, to your subscribers, you will start seeing your email traffic increase over time. As we'll talk about in the next chapter, the people on your email list will be the greatest source of income for your business, and links inside of emails will be an excellent way to get people back to your site.

Another tip to increase your email traffic is to include a "call-to-action" in every email you write. Have a goal for your message before you hit send, and have a reason for everyone who reads that email to click a link, come back to your site, or hit "reply." I didn't do this very well in the beginning, but as I started to clarify my brand and message, developing these calls to action became easier. Sometimes the action you want subscribers to take is "read more," other times it's "leave a comment" and others still, it's "click here to buy now."

If you're creating new content on a regular basis, making each new post and page search engine friendly, sharing your work on social media and making real connections through guest posting and interviews, there is no way your business won't grow. While it may not explode overnight, each of these strategies will help you build a network of searchable content, a web of quality backlinks, and following on social media that will help establish a solid foundation from which your business can grow.

Lastly, the key ingredient in getting more traffic and building an audience, the one thing that cannot be overlooked and cannot go unmentioned, is high-quality content. Without great content, no amount of optimization, social sharing or emailing will help you build your online business.

As David Ogilvy, the "father of advertising," once said, "Great marketing only makes a bad product fail faster." If you're not making the best possible content, creating experiences that wow,[29] and over delivering to your customers, no amount of promotion will help you.

---

[29] See *Over Delivering and Creating Experiences that Wow!* - https://www.ellorywells.com/experiences-that-wow/

On the flip side, creating the best possible product that helps people, meets their needs, solves their problems and makes their life better is the best way to build a good reputation online. When someone reads your post, listens to your podcast, eats at your restaurant or uses your product in a way that makes their life better, they're much more likely to tell people about it than if their experience was just mediocre. Amaze and delight your customers and they'll do the marketing for you.

One bonus tip before we move on. Most people don't know about this trick, but I want to share it with you.

If you sign up for both Google's[30] and Bing's[31] Webmaster Tools, you can submit your blog's sitemaps (which Yoast SEO can generate for you) directly to the search engines. Instead of sitting around waiting for Google and Bing to catalog and index your site, you can submit a request directly to them.

Like the card catalog at a library, search engines keep a directory of every website they index. This index is a good indication of what content is on a site, the keywords, the inbound and outbound links, the authors, posts, and pages. By submitting your sitemaps to Google and Bing, you're essentially telling them, "Hey, look over here and check out my website!"

It's a pretty nifty trick if you ask me. I submit my sitemaps almost every week, and that process has helped my search traffic grow significantly over the past few years.

---

[30] Sign up for a free Google Webmaster Tools account at https://www.google.com/webmasters/

[31] Sign up for a free Bing Webmaster Tools account at https://www.bing.com/toolbox/webmaster

Word of Mouth

Finally, and I almost left this one off because it's very similar to referrals, let's talk about the value of word of mouth advertising.

A few years ago, right before I started my first major podcast, I had the chance to meet and shake the hand of one of the godfathers of podcasting, Cliff Ravenscraft. At the time, my focus was on the money - how to not spend it, but how to make it.

I knew Cliff had made quite a lot of money podcasting and teaching others to do the same, so, when the opportunity presented itself, I asked Cliff, "How do I make money with my podcast?"

Cliff thought about my question and answered with something I wasn't expecting. He said, "Ellory, you're asking the wrong question. Don't focus on making money, focus on creating value."

And then Cliff said something I hope I never forget.

He said, "Be so good they can't ignore you."

When you're worried about getting traffic, whether it's visitors to your blog, listeners to your podcast, viewers to your YouTube channel, or people walking into your store, remember Steve Martin's advice that Cliff passed on to me. Be so good that people want to keep coming back for more. Be so good that no one can ignore the fact that you exist. And, be so good they want to tell their friends and family so that they, too, can benefit from what you have to offer.

27: HOW TO BUILD YOUR EMAIL LIST

*I hear YouTube, Twitter and Facebook are merging to
form a super Social Media site – YouTwitFace.*
- Conan O'Brien

Traffic to your website is fantastic, but subscribers are better. As I mentioned in Week 2 of the Roadmap, there's a saying in internet marketing that says, "The money is in the list." Well, the "list" is your list of everyone who enters their email address and subscribes to updates from your website.

If the money is in the list, the next logical questions are, "How do I build and grow my list?" and "How big of a list do I need?" That's what this chapter is about, converting the traffic to your site from visitors to subscribers. Later we'll look at how to turn those subscribers into customers.

There are three types of visitors to your site: the interested, the involved, and the invested. Your goal is to attract each type and offer something to entice them into subscribing. Once they're on your list, your job is to move them through the process from casual reader to paying customer. Without paying customers, your exit strategy won't work. It's not always about the money, but you've got to pay the bills.

In the spirit of full disclosure, I must admit that it took me eighteen months to get my first fifty subscribers. I didn't know what I'm about to share with you, and it was a slow process. It took me ten months to get my second fifty, and another five months to bust through 150.

When you're starting out, growing your email list can be slow but you'll no doubt build momentum. When you serve your subscribers, deliver exclusive content, and provide value, they'll tell their friends and keep coming back. By the way, to go from 150 to over 200 subscribers took me less than ninety days.

Let's look at how we target the three types of people who will visit your site.

3 Types of People Who Follow Your Business

The Interested

People who visit your site and who fall into the "interested" category are the casual observers. They're the ones who read a post and bounce (bounce is the technical term for visiting a single page and leaving; I'm not going thug on you).

The interested people, if they decide to come back or stick around, are the ones who would be interested in "joining a community" or "getting updates" from your website. They don't want to miss out on what's going on, but they're not ready to become involved or invested.

By putting an opt-in box in your site's footer, you can capture these interested leads with language like "Enter your email to get updates" or "Join the Community." When you're first starting and don't have a ton of content to draw people in, opt-in boxes like these are a perfect way to start.

The interested people are at the very top of your sales funnel and aren't sure if they want to buy from you or get involved with what you're doing.

The Involved

Your visitors who are in the "involved" category are the ones who sign up for webinars, opt-in for reports and ebooks, and who trade their email address for what you know. Involved people haven't spent money with you, but they engage with you via email and social media. They want access to how-to guides, comparisons or industry reports, templates you've created. The "involved" people in your audience comprise the group from which you'll make your first dollars. They're the ones most likely to buy or who are about to buy.

Involved people are the warm leads for your business. They're actively engaged and eager for more. Yes, they're interested in the community too, and want to get updates, but they also want to get involved and interact with like-minded people.

You can attract visitors who wish to be involved with what you're doing by placing an opt-in box on the sidebar of your site, above the fold (i.e. visible without having to scroll down). You could also attract them with resource downloads or transcripts from within your posts. Involved people want to "download the report" or "get these resources" and are likely to take action when you use that type of language.

The involved people are in the middle of your sales funnel. They know and like you, but they're not quite ready to trust you and invest their money with you. Once they buy, they become invested.

The Invested

People who have spent money or are currently spending money with you are "invested." They're invested in themselves and in their future, and they're investing in you and your product. Invested people in your audience are the ones you can thank every time you swipe your debit card. They help you keep the lights on and provide you with the capital required to purchase better tools and grow your business.

While opt-in boxes to become invested can work, they often don't. In my experience, the people in my audience who spend money with me were interested and involved first. The more brand recognition you have, the faster people will go from interested to invested, but they'll still go through each phase.

Most people want to know, like and trust you before they'll spend money with you. If you've given away free, high-quality resources for long enough, they'll believe that you can deliver the results they're looking for. There are only two ways to build credibility with someone; you either build it or borrow it. When you're starting, you'll have to build it one person at a time.

You can encourage your visitors to become invested by offering free coaching calls, open office hours, samples of your product and "ask me anything" styled question and answer sessions that showcase your skills. These types of things are a proof of concept - they allow people to see what you can do and what level of value you can provide. The more value you can provide up front and for free, the less time you'll have to spend selling people on your value on the back end.

To summarize, the "interested" people are the ones who want to be kept in the loop about what you're doing. The "involved" are the people who interact with your content, send you emails, engage with you on social media and take your free courses. Once someone pays, they're no longer "involved," but become "invested."

Now that you know the types of people who follow your business let's look at some basic "bribes" you can deploy to encourage people to sign up for your list.

Why People Subscribe

Few people will be willing to hand over their email address for no reason. In today's world, where the average person receives dozens if not hundreds of emails each day, it's increasingly difficult to get people to sign up for your email list. While that can be frustrating, it's for a reason. People have downloaded too many lackluster "free ebooks" and worthless "industry reports" to be eager to opt-in for yours. Especially if they don't yet know, like or trust you.

The good news is, at a time when free ebooks are a dime a dozen, it's easy to stand out if you're willing to put in the extra effort. By researching, spending additional time polishing and designing, and delivering a free resource that adds incredible value or actionable advice, you can stand out from everyone else who is offering a free PDF download. You'll have to show people you're different before they'll opt-in, but you're not afraid of a little work, are you?

Here are some of the most common types of "bribes" for which people are often willing to subscribe.

- **Checklists** - Beginners love checklists. If you can provide a foolproof list of things the pros use, people who want to be like those pros will subscribe to get it. My checklist of professional podcasting gear for beginners is a reader favorite.[32]

---

[32] Check out my podcast checklist at https://www.ellorywells.com/lp/download-mobile-podcast-studio-gear/

- **Ebooks** - Everyone loves a downloadable ebook. One of the most popular ebook opt-ins is *eBooks the Smart Way* written by Pat Flynn of SmartPassiveIncome.com. [33] Pat over-delivered with his bribe and tens of thousands of people have subscribed to his list because of it.

- **Guides** - Guides are an excellent way to illustrate your expertise and help solve problems. If you can walk people through the solution to a problem, they'll love you for it. To create your guide, solve a problem, document the process, and share the steps with your audience. They'll opt-in by the truckload.

- **Exclusives** - Everyone wants to be a VIP. If you have an exclusive interview to share, a behind-the-scenes look, or information you only share with your community, people will subscribe.

People opt-in because they want to feel included, and they're afraid of missing out. They subscribe because they believe you can shorten their learning curve, reduce their startup time, provide them with discounts or coupons, or other items of exclusive value. Visitors want you to help them eliminate their pain, and they're willing to trade their email address for it. If you can help your audience add more tools to their tool belt or make their life easier, they'll subscribe to your list.

---

[33] Check out Pat Flynn's ebook at http://www.smartpassiveincome.com/ebooks-the-smart-way/

Advanced Techniques to Entice Subscribers

Now, let's look at some more advanced techniques you can use to draw people in and grow your email list. If you're just starting or have little to no content, you may want to read this part and take notes so you can come back to it again later. On the other hand, if you can implement these tactics, you'll be able to launch with explosive force from the beginning.

These advanced list building techniques require more work, time, and skill to pull off, but their results are worth it.

Email Courses

I had never heard of an email course until I found the "Email1k" course [34] from Noah Kagan and the team at AppSumo. After enrolling, the course content was delivered directly to my inbox. Every week I'd get an email full of information, tips and tricks. No need to click a link or go elsewhere, everything I needed was right in my inbox.

I loved the concept so much I created my own email course in 2014 called *The 30 Day Blog Transformation*. [35] Using my free course, I get to teach people around the world with lessons like How to Think Like a Successful Entrepreneur, How to Identify Your Ideal Client and Maximize Your Impact (and Profit!), The 5 Pages that Convert Your Blog Into a Booming Business, Why NOW is the Best Time in HISTORY to Be an Entrepreneur and Make a Global Impact, and The Most Powerful Momentum-Builder for Your Beginner Business.

---

[34] Find out more and enroll at http://email1k.com/

[35] Check out my free email course and enroll at https://www.ellorywells.com/lp/30-day-blog-transformation/

Every month new people join my email list to get access to these lessons and join our community of writers. Using the "Email1k" framework, in addition to emailing each lesson, I have posted each lesson on a unique site where students of the course can post comments and ask questions. I also have a private Facebook group for students and alumni who want to interact with one another.

Webinars

Webinars, short for "web-seminars," are lessons taught through online video streaming where a host shares information with an audience. If you promise to teach your webinar attendees something valuable, people will opt in to claim their seat at the virtual table.

John Lee Dumas of EntrepreneurOnFire.com has used webinars to add hundreds of thousands of dollars in revenue to his business. He teaches audience members enough about podcasting to help them get started, then offers a premium product at the end for anyone looking for additional help. Remember the "freemium" model we explored in Chapter 13? Webinars are a perfect execution of that strategy.

If you're interested in learning about the best tools and resources for hosting webinars, I invite you to check out a video interview I did for my membership site. I had the chance to speak with Jon Shumacher, author of *Hangouts Marketing Mastery*, about how to use webinars to build an email list, attract new clients and increase your revenue. I invite you to become a member at www.theexitstrategybook.com/offer and get access to the full interview with Jon.

Giveaways

During each quarter of the year, I try to hold a giveaway to build my email list. I pick three to five books, products or services that have helped me, and I bundle them together as a giveaway.

The first giveaway I held included Jeff Goins' book *The In-Between*. After promoting the giveaway on social media, I caught the attention of Jeff himself, who shared and retweeted about the giveaway to his audience. I had hundreds of people check out the giveaway and share it with their networks.

Online tools like KingSumo's Giveaways plugin for Wordpress[36] and Rafflecopter[37] make it easy to create giveaways and grow your email list. All you have to do is choose an item or items you want to give away and require an email address to enter to win. Both services pick a random winner and allow you to add the entrants to your list of subscribers. Participants have a chance to win a free item, and you have a new person on your list.

If you try one of these strategies, and it doesn't work the first time, don't give up! A good portion of success is about testing, tweaking and retesting, to see what works. Your audience may respond to one of these strategies and but not another. The key to growing your email list is to always have something valuable for which people are willing to trade their email address.

Let's now take a look at the five key ingredients to a killer opt-in. After all, knowing what types of things visitors are looking for is essential to getting them on your list!

Designing the Perfect Lead Magnet

Every business wants more leads. But, few companies understand what goes into creating a lead magnet that will convert visitors to prospects. Your goal with a lead magnet is to convert visitors to

---

36 Find out more at https://kingsumo.com/apps/giveaways/
37 Find out more at https://www.rafflecopter.com/

leads, leads to customers, and customers to raving fans and repeat buyers. That process is what enables every business to grow.

These are the five key criteria of a lead magnet that converts visitors into subscribers and customers.

Provide a Specific Solution to a Specific Person

Your lead magnet should target a specific person, or type of person, with the promise of specific results. Your lead magnet should not try to attract everybody. If you try to reach everyone, you'll connect with no one.

By speaking to a specific person, your "avatar," you're talking to the ideal person who will get the most value and best results from what you're offering. When you offer to provide a specific outcome, potential new leads will know exactly what they'll get in exchange for their email address. Most mammals run from uncertainty, so be specific and tell your visitors precisely what they'll get from your lead magnet. If you know who you're trying to attract and what you're going to deliver when you create your lead magnet, the other key criteria will fall into place.

Deliver One (Epic) Result

Instead of promising to give a dozen ways to build something better or faster, focus on delivering the absolute best way. Instead of offering to give someone a complete marketing plan, offer the one thing they can do to get more followers on Twitter, likes on Facebook, or friends on LinkedIn. If you target people who want to grow their influence on Facebook, you'll attract more subscribers than if you target social media as a whole. Focus your lead magnet and provide one epic result.

Create Immediate Results or a Quick Fix

Your lead magnet should be the "ace in the hole," your "silver bullet," or your "#1 tip" to get the job done. In today's world, people are looking for shortcuts. They want that one key thing that will move the needle for them. If they can help it, your subscribers aren't interested in working for hours on end to get results; they want something they can put into place now.

If you've been working on an ebook for your giveaway or "bribe," you can take a break. I've just given you pretty good news. Set your book aside and create a one or two-page download of your best stuff.

Deliver High Value

Your lead magnet is often the first impression someone gets when trying to decide if they want to join your community. Use the initial opt-in as your opportunity to provide over-the-top value. Your lead magnet is your chance to blow their mind with how much valuable information you have to give them.

Over deliver. Do more for your new subscriber than they're expecting and help them get better results than they'd hoped. Not only will they stick with you, but they'll be well on their way to becoming a raving fan.

Have a Transformational Effect

An epic lead magnet should have a transformational effect on the people who sign up for it. The information contained within your lead magnet should move your new subscriber from where they are to where they want to be. It should change their thinking from "is that even possible" to "wow, this is happening!"

Think back to the last lead magnet for which you traded your email. The best ones, the lead magnets we remember and share with our friends, are the ones that give us a "wow" moment and open our eyes to new possibilities. Epic lead magnets show us new ways of thinking and transport us from where we were, to where we are, and to where we want to go. In other words, your lead magnet should transform us from who we are to who we want to be.

Now that you know the five key elements of an epic lead magnet let's look at how you can convert all of those new subscribers into paying customers.

28: CREATING CUSTOMERS

Don't optimize for conversions, optimize for revenue.
- Neil Patel

If you had a Facebook page for your business in the middle of 2013, you could get your posts and messages in front of 13-20% of your audience. Whenever you posted an update to your page, a decent number of the people who "like" your page would see what you shared in their newsfeed and interact with it.

Toward the end of 2013, Facebook made a change to their algorithm. Now, instead of double-digit exposure, you'd be lucky to get 4% of your audience to see your posts. This is just one example and one reason why online entrepreneurs say "the money is in the list" and why you shouldn't depend on social media to build your business.

What you should focus on is how to convert your subscribers into customers. In this chapter, we'll look at ways you can do that.

Getting Customers to Know, Like & Trust You

All things being equal, we buy from businesses we know, like and trust. Consumers want to know about business and what they do. They want to like the business' reputation, products, and services. And before they buy, they must trust that the company can deliver a valuable solution. Here's how you can get your customers to know, like and trust you so your business can grow and thrive.

Know

Before anyone can interact with you, they first must know you exist. But converting subscribers to paying customers goes beyond that. They have to know who you are, what you're about, and what you stand for. Then and only then, will they be open to purchasing what you have to offer. These two obstacles are opportunities in disguise, so let's take a closer look.

Knowing you first comes from knowing you exist. Before someone can buy from you, they must also know where to find you. If a prospect has never heard of you or what services you provide, how can they ever get to know you? Well, they can't. Remember, you have the glass of water thirsty people everywhere are looking for, but you must let them know you're there and have what they need

The second part of your customers knowing who you are is knowing your principles, what made you who you are, and your beliefs. In general, consumers buy from people and companies who are like them and share similar beliefs.

When Chick-fil-A made public statements about their position on same-sex marriage in 2012,[38] they told the world what they believed and what they were about. The people who believed like Chick-fil-A continued to buy from them and the people who disagreed took their business elsewhere.

I'm not advocating that you make public statements about your religious or political beliefs, but I'm telling you it's a good idea to have an About Page that tells your story and how you see the world. Your audience wants to know who you are. They want to know where you're from, where you went to school, and what type of work you do. Prospective customers want to know the journey you've taken to get where you are so they can feel confident about your ability to help them.

Politics and religion aside, your audience wants to know what you believe and why you believe it. If you take a firm stand that everyone should be using social media as their primary marketing tool, you better be able to articulate why and support your statement with facts, experiences, or past results. If you believe that WordPress is the website builder of the future, or that podcasting is the best connection tool since the telegraph, you'd better be able to stand behind those statements.

If you share your views with your audience, two things will happen. The people who believe as you do will stick around and support you. And the people who don't think like you will either go somewhere else or stay and heckle you. In either case, your beliefs will bring people to your corner, and that's a good thing.

Once people get to know you and have a decent idea of where your head is at, they can start to like you.

---

[38] Source: https://en.wikipedia.org/wiki/Chick-fil-A_same-sex_marriage_controversy

Like

Have you ever stopped to think about the people you hang out with? Have you ever wondered why you enjoy spending so much time with them? Beyond that, have you ever thought about how you became friends with them in the first place?

I hope you haven't started checking your friends off any lists or deleting them from your phone just yet. But the questions about why people like you, and why you like them, are worth asking, especially when it applies to you growing your business.

We're friends with our friends because they (usually) believe the same things we believe. If you look at the people you hang out with the most, they probably have similar political and religious views. They probably enjoy the same types of movies and television shows, and you might even like reading the same books.

This is natural. Communities are made up of people who have the same worldviews. We stick together for survival, and we agree so we can get along. When we get along, we are much more likely to succeed and survive than if we were fighting or arguing all of the time.

Additionally, we're friends with our friends because their quirks amuse us. The goofy things our friends do are often the same things that cause us to like them. We like Star Wars but not Star Trek. We don't eat meat, and we love to go hiking. We vote conservative and go to church on Sunday. These are the unique things about us that help us form the bonds necessary to develop friendships.

When it comes to your brand, these same quirks will help you connect with people around the world and help you build your tribe. When I first started in the online world, I tried to hide my goofiness. I didn't talk about my love for science fiction and video games. But as I learned more about connecting with people and building relationships, I realized that the reason people liked me *offline* were the same reasons why people would like me *online*.

Then, when your audience sees that not only do you have the same beliefs and worldviews they do, but you also like the same shows and movies, a connection is made at a deeper level. If someone knows you, they will say hello to you on the street. If they like you, they'll meet you for lunch. If they trust you, they'll invite you to their home for dinner.

Trust

When people trust you, they're willing to partner with you. Sometimes that partnership means asking for your advice, other times it means trading their money for your products and services. So, how do you get people to trust you?

In today's world, one where anyone and everyone with an internet connection can start a website, it can be overwhelming to think about developing trust with someone half a planet away.

It's possible. And necessary. The good thing is, you can start building trust with someone even while they're still deciding whether or not they like you in the first place.

Getting someone to trust you is pretty simple. Not only are most people trusting by nature, but it's easier to make a real connection today than ever before. Even though the number of people online is increasing every year, the number willing to be open, honest, authentic and transparent isn't.

You build trust with your audience every time you share a piece of your story. Every time you talk about where you grew up, you build trust. Each time you tell a story about the crazy things you did in school, you build trust. The stories you tell that give people a look at your life *offline* will help people know, like and trust you *online*. Weird how that works, huh?

You also build trust by sharing the parts of your business that don't go according to plan. This is where you can stand out from the crowd if you're willing to be vulnerable and let people in. If you only talk about things that go perfectly, people won't believe you because we know we all make mistakes. But, if you can share the things that don't work, people will relate to you even more.

Imagine the following scenario and think about which person you'd relate to more. Imagine Martha in her stainless steel kitchen with great lighting and the latest technology in ovens and cookware. With all of that fancy equipment, is there any doubt she can bake a perfect cake!

Now imagine Susan, who has three kids and is doing her best to put food on the table. On screen, she invites you into her home and shows you how to make a delicious meal with the pots and pans you already have in your kitchen and the food you're likely to have in your pantry. Her cake doesn't look quite as good as Martha's, but it tastes delicious and makes the kids smile with joy.

Now, ask yourself this question, "who did you relate to more, Martha or Susan, and why?"

Most likely you connect with Susan because she's more like you, or you have similar backgrounds and life stories. No one is perfect, so when we share our imperfections, we show that we're real. Perfect people and perfect lives aren't real people or real lives.

If you want people to trust you, show your strengths and your weaknesses. Show your audience your flaws and how you're working through them. It's counterintuitive, but showing people you aren't perfect is one of the best ways to get them to know, like and trust you.

Tripwires

During Week 8 of the Roadmap, we spent a fair bit of time talking about emails and email marketing, but we're not done. Now let's discuss the tactic of the tripwire - the tool deployed right after an opt-in but before the first email. The tripwire is designed to grab someone's attention with an incredible offer and convert them to a paying customer.

My current tripwire is a 93% discount on my membership site. Instead of paying $34 each month, a new subscriber can get three months for $7. This isn't my only offer, but it's one of the best.

A good tripwire is designed to take advantage of forward motion. After a new visitor comes to your website and decides they want your free offer (lead magnet), the tripwire keeps them moving toward being a customer, turning one yes into another, and another, and another.

Think about the products and services you have to offer. Your tripwire should align with your goal and move people who are *interested* in your business through the process so they become *invested* in what you have.

When I first started, I didn't have a tripwire. Even after I created my first one, it didn't quite move people in the direction I wanted. Here's a good example of a tripwire that's in near-perfect alignment with the business's goal.

I have a chiropractor as one of my clients. After we started working together, his business grew exponentially. His success serves as an example of how what you're reading here is relevant in the offline world as well. One of his lead magnets was a free adjustment and a health evaluation. My client knows that obscurity is one of the biggest challenges facing a new business. To combat that obstacle, he removes a reason for someone to not visit. If he can get them in the door, he can get them to come back.

To keep his new patient's forward momentum, my client offers a loyalty card as a tripwire. After six visits, your seventh adjustment is free.

Why six?

After looking at his patient data, my client realized that if a patient visits him six times, they almost always continue as a patient for a year, sometimes more. Six visits is a critical point, so my client incentivizes the patient with a complimentary adjustment to get them in the door, then offers them the tripwire as an incentive to keep coming back.

When considering your tripwire, think about the path an interested person would likely take before making the decision to buy. If your goal is to sign a new client, what thought processes will they go through to get there? If you want to be the preferred Friday night hot spot in your town, what objections are keeping that from happening?

Have in mind the ideal action you want your clients to take and work backward from there. Your tripwire should all but eliminate the first hurdle and get your future customer moving toward the decision you want them to make. Get them to say yes, then encourage their forward momentum with another valuable offer.

The Emails

Now let's look at how you can use email marketing to get your audience to know, like and trust you, and how you can convert subscribers into paying customers.

The best way to turn subscribers into customers is by providing value each and every time you hit send. Just because you're sending an email instead of publishing a post doesn't mean you get off easy and can forget about why you're writing it in the first place.

When I worked at Dell, I received 300-400 emails a day from customers. According to the marketing and technology research firm Radicati, the average person gets somewhere around 220 emails a day across all of their accounts.[39] What's worse, almost 15% of those emails aren't wanted and considered spam.

As an online business owner and email marketer, those numbers should scare and motivate you. They should cause fear because the email you just poured lots of thought into might not get

---

[39] Radicati Email Statistics Report, 2014-2018: http://www.radicati.com/wp-content/uploads/2014/01/Email-Statistics-Report-2014-2018-Executive-Summary.pdf

read. Those statistics should motivate you to write the best possible email and the most value possible before you hit send. You can do those things by having a reason for every single email you send or every automated email you add to your autoresponder series.

When writing your emails, consider why someone would want to open it. Is your subject line descriptive and compelling? Does it entice people to read the rest of the email? Is content of your message relevant to your subscribers and related to why they signed up to your list? Does the preview of the email tell your subscriber enough that they know what they're about to open and be curious and eager? These are just a few things to think about before you hit send.

Think about what they'll get by reading your email. Will they have new information and feel compelled to take an action? Will your subscriber get to know you and your background more? Will they learn about a new tool or resource that will help them?

We're all busy, and if you can make your subscriber's life easier or better with your email, then do it. Then, when you've added enough value over time, they'll keep opening your emails and be more likely to make a purchase.

Consider what action you want your subscriber to take after reading your email. By having a call to action at the beginning, middle and end of your email, you guide your subscriber to the desired action. Sometimes the call to action, or CTA, is "click here to learn more." Other times it's "click here to buy now" or "click here to download this resource." Whatever your CTA is, make sure it's clear to understand and easy to perform.

The Message

If you're following these guidelines and writing compelling subject lines with valuable content in the emails, you'll begin the process of converting subscribers to customers. But what do those emails need to say? What should you write about? Let's take a look.

As with the story of Martha and Susan from earlier in this chapter, your subscribers want to hear your story. They want to know what tools you use so they can use them too. And, they want to know how to get the best deals on your products and services.

If you remember from the last chapter, your audience is divided into three categories: the interested, the involved and the invested. Your subscribers also follow the same pattern; some of them are merely interested in what you're up to, others are eager to interact, while others still are hungry to invest in what you have to offer.

By sharing additional details with your subscribers via email, you're telling them you were just like them when you started. Then, in the next email, you can show them how far you've come and what tools you used to get there. Finally, your third email tells your subscriber they can be like you, learn how you did it, and learn from you if they choose.

Boom, there's your email marketing plan and how you convert subscribers to paying customers. If people buy from the people they know, like and trust, with three emails, you've accomplished that go. You've shown them that A) you're a real person, B) how you did what you did, and C) how you can help them get similar results.

But let me warn you, none of this happens overnight. It takes time to grow your list. It takes time to write the content of your email marketing campaigns. It takes time to cultivate trust. And, it requires even more time to create the products to sell to the people on that list.

Some experts will tell you to lead with a product; others will tell you to follow your passion. I'm going to advise that you do a combination of both and apply this suggestion to both your email subscribers and your blog readers alike.

On one hand, you can't sell a product if you don't have one. On the other, your passion could lead you somewhere that isn't profitable. Many things about business are trial and error so keep testing. If you're not passionate about the product you do have to sell, you'll never be able to build a business you love. And loving your business is the whole point, right?

Indoctrination

Part of converting your "interested" subscribers, samplers, and people who are just browsing into "invested" customers, is influencing them to believe as you do. They need to believe that you have the best book, the best food, the best crafting supplies, the best deals, etc., so they feel comfortable spending their money with you instead of with someone else.

To accomplish this task, you need some sort of indoctrination process. This could be a price match guarantee. It could be customer reviews or pictures of celebrities who've visited your restaurant hanging on the wall.

In the online world, your indoctrination comes in the way of a carefully designed series of emails meant to introduce your brand to the target and turn a stranger into a friend who knows, likes and trusts you.

My indoctrination series currently has three parts. I'll show you what I've got, but if you really want to become an expert and create your own set of indoctrination emails, I highly recommend Ryan Deiss's book *Invisible Selling Machine: 5 Steps to Crafting an Automated, Evergreen Email Campaign that Literally Makes Sales While You Sleep.*

Before I share what I say in my emails, take a look at the following image.

This is a screenshot of part of my indoctrination series of emails taken from inside my ActiveCampaign automation.

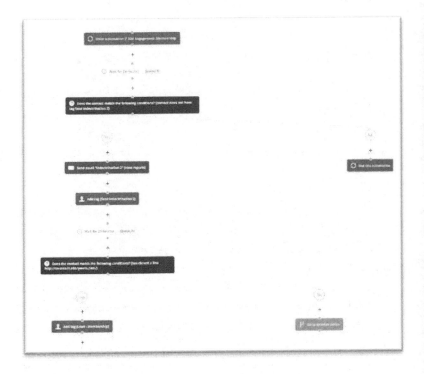

New subscribers start at the top and progress downward through a series of emails, waiting periods, and conditional checkpoints.

Indoctrination Email #1

The first email in the series welcomes people to my community and thanks them for subscribing. I immediately mention that the tool or resource they opted in for is on its way, but I ask them to first add me to their list of safe senders. I also provide a link to instructions on how to do that.

I also tell them what they can expect from me. The types of content, the kinds of emails, and the characteristics of people who generally find the most value in what I have to say.

Lastly, I outline what I'll be sending them next, and ask them to connect with me on social media. I provide links to Facebook, Twitter, LinkedIn, and other places where I'm active.

About five minutes after Indoctrination Email #1, I send them the email containing a link to download the resource for which they opted in.

Indoctrination Email #2

After greeting the subscriber by name, I open the email thanking them, again, for spending time with me. Then, I reference the email I sent them yesterday, A) so they know I did, and B) so they can go read it if they haven't already.

The main reason I send this email is to share my story. I want my subscribers to know that I'm a lot like them, and anything I've done, they can do too. My audience is largely do-it-yourself entrepreneurs, so I try to connect with them where they are and show them we're a lot alike. If I can do it, so can they, etc.

Toward the end of the email, I mention what services I offer and who typically signs up to work with me. Finally, before signing off, I ask them again to connect on social media, and I share what I'll be sending them next, in indoctrination email #3.

Indoctrination Email #3

On the third day someone is on my list, they get my third email. While we shouldn't try to bombard our new subscribers with emails, we need to be mindful of the fact that the days immediately following the initial opt-in are when a person's interest in us is at its highest.

In this third email, I thank them again for being on my list and reiterate what I'll be sending them in the future. It's a brief statement of gratitude and intent in case they haven't read (or received) my other emails.

My third indoctrination email also includes a photo with social proof. I include a picture taken at a meetup I held in 2015. This picture not only says, "Hey, I'm a real person!" but it also says, "Hey, see, there are other people that think I'm pretty cool too. You're in good company!" Social proof is an incredibly powerful thing, so I make sure it's front and center in email #3.

Following the picture of my meetup, I share how people can dive into my content. I share links to popular blog posts and podcast episodes and mention the posting schedule I try to keep on a weekly basis.

Finally, before wrapping up, and as I always try to do, I close with a question asking the subscriber if there is any way I can help them.

The last bit of the email reinforces the fact that I'll be emailing them again down the road, asks them again to whitelist my email address, and one more final attempt to get them to follow me on social media.

After the third email, each subscriber is then transferred to my general autoresponder automation where I send them emails approximately every week for several weeks. The emails in that series are designed to provide value, increase engagement, and drive traffic. The content of those emails follows a meandering path of give value, value, value, ask for a favor.

If all this sounds like a lot, it is. But, it takes a lot of work to build a business.

The good thing about your indoctrination series is that A) you don't have to retype or recreate the emails very often, and B) once you get a system in place, it works for you, behind the scenes, converting subscribers into customers.

Email marketing is as much art as it is science. If you want to know what I know, go straight to the source and check out the book *Invisible Selling Machine* by Ryan Deiss and get the information direct from one of the best marketers I've ever met.

29: HOW TO SELL YOUR PRODUCTS (AND FEEL GOOD ABOUT IT)

If you believe in what you are doing, then let nothing hold you up in your work.
- Dale Carnegie

I didn't grow up in a family of entrepreneurs. You could argue that my dad was an entrepreneur, but unless you consider insurance agents who sell for major corporations as "entrepreneurs," he wasn't.

In fact, my family is the least entrepreneurial family I can think of. On my mom's side, there are several generations of teachers, principals, superintendents and football coaches. On my dad's, there are insurance salesmen and pharmaceutical sales reps. Both branches of the family tree are deeply rooted in working for the man and doing as you're told. Sorry family members, I love you, but you didn't prepare me to start my own business.

So, when I say I had to learn how to create and sell my own products and figure out how to build a business on my own, I mean it. The only thing I've ever done that you might consider as entrepreneurship is the "detective agency" my sister and I started when we were both under ten years old. I think the only detecting we did was go looking for a missing fountain pen or the neighbor's lost cat.

But not having a history of business ownership in your family shouldn't keep you from pursuing your dream of building a business you love. Let's take a look at the mindset required for you to be successful selling your products and how you can feel good about it instead of feeling like a slimy used car salesman.

The only way you can create your own product and successfully sell it is by believing that your product will make a difference in the life of the person who uses it. If your product doesn't change someone, what's the point? No matter how small the widget or minor the service, your product must make a difference.

Before any sort of intimidation, self-doubt or fear sets in, consider the difference a sip of water can have to a thirsty person. Or, consider how grateful you were for that tiny package of pretzels or peanuts when you were starving on a long flight. And think about how much you'd pay to get access to a European toilet when you really need to go (not to mention usable toilet paper). The amount of impact your product has on the world has nothing to do with its size or cost.

And that's a good thing, too. Since we don't have to worry about creating a large, expensive product to have a significant impact on the people around us, we also don't have to worry about high startup costs, manufacturing space, or anything else that would go along with creating a large and expensive product. This also means we can start, build and grow our business from where we are and with what we have.

I love the analogy of water for thirsty people; it applies so well to creating services and building a business.

To sell your product and feel good about it, you have to see thirsty people everywhere. They're thirsty for something better.

They're thirsty and are on the lookout for something to drink - something you have.

If your product doesn't have a particular person whom it will impact, it will not sell. And, is it wrong to be a water salesman in the desert? No, that's capitalism. And that's what entrepreneurs do; we see the needs of the people and find a way to meet those needs. Entrepreneurs provide a quality service or product to the people who need it in exchange for payment so they can continue providing it to someone else who needs it tomorrow.

Think back to the last time you were hungry. I mean starving, like, you hadn't eaten in hours, and you were about to start gnawing on your arm. When you finally found something to eat, did you ask for the food for free? Were you upset at the person selling the food or angry that they were profiting off of your situation?

No, you weren't. Most likely you were grateful to them for making the food available and were more than willing to pay them for their time and effort.

The reason I've spent the last few pages focused on this idea of meeting needs and profiting is that the exchange is foreign and uncomfortable to a lot of people. Sure, we're more than willing to be on the consumer side of the transaction, and we don't see anything wrong with it. But, from the producer and business owner side, for some reason, we feel like we're not worthy of charging or we feel bad about it when we do.

Until you believe you have what people need, and what you possess is worth charging for, you will never be able to build a business. What's worse, not believing in yourself and your product will result in you undercharging for what you have to offer. This makes people less likely to buy, which makes you lower your prices. And so goes the vicious cycle until you go out of business.

If everyone wanted cheap products, companies like Mercedes, Lexus, and Acura wouldn't exist, even less likely are brands like Ferrari and Porsche. And until you find where your products fit, it will be difficult to sell them.

The bottom line is this: is what you're creating the best it can be? Every time you hit publish or print, each time you ship your widget or take your pie out of the oven, do you know it will help someone?

30: FINDING YOUR IDEAL AVATAR

To market a product or service properly, the first thing
you must do is get clear on who your ideal customer is,
where they are hanging out, what their challenges are…
- Russ Henneberry

If you try to reach everyone with your message, you won't connect with anyone. It almost seems counterintuitive, but the more focused you are with your product, service or message, the more people you'll actually have an impact on. It's like a punch versus a slap; when you concentrate, you'll have more force than if you were spread too thin.

When I began blogging in 2012, I wasn't writing to anyone in particular. I had no focus. Looking back on that time now, I can say that I was likely writing to my co-workers at Dell. Or, at least to people like them.

Most content creators who fail do the same things I did in the beginning, and they don't make the changes I'm about to share with you. The entrepreneurs who succeed, the ones who build a successful business, are the ones who put the these strategies into place and use them as a social barometer for their product and service creation efforts.

Over the last few years, I've taken a mental note of the new bloggers, podcasters and entrepreneurs I meet. All of them want to change the world, most of them have a message, and many of them have a plan. However, few of them know who they're talking to. Almost none of them have invested the time to figuring out their ideal client avatar.

Time spent understanding your avatar is time well invested. Once you know what your ideal clients need, you can provide it to them. After you've determined what challenges they'll have, you can offer accurate solutions.

If you know your avatar is a vegan female, you know you can stop worrying about keeping hamburgers on the menu. If your avatar is a recent college graduate male, you don't have to worry about keeping tampons on the shelves.

By identifying your avatar, you can be more effective with your marketing and more efficient with your budget. When you target a particular type of person, these people will feel like you're talking directly to them, or, that you're making your products specifically for them.

Finding your ideal client avatar will help you waste less money, make more profit, and get more done in less time. Sound like a plan?

In the following section, we'll define the term "avatar," and I will show you how to get as clear and concrete about who that person is. I'll walk you through the same process I went through a few years ago and that I take all of my coaching clients through now. I'll also show you how your avatar, whether it's a he or she, differs from your "audience" and how you can build your business around marketing to both.

What is an Avatar?

Though initially a Hindu term used to refer to a deity who took physical form, the word avatar has a different meaning in business. However, the way we use avatar today still has roots in its origins.

In the business world today, your avatar is a particular person, or type of person, who is the best possible buyer of your products or services. They're the ones who will get the most use out of it, connect with your message the most, and who will feel most connected with your brand. Your avatar is the person who knows, likes and trusts you the quickest because they're needs are in perfect alignment with your message.

Still unclear?

Your avatar is made up of everything you know about your ideal customer. Your avatar is the mental picture (or literal one) of the person you're writing, podcasting, and creating for. The details that make up your avatar are things like their age, where they live, their likes and dislikes, what they buy and who they buy from. The more you know about your avatar, the better you can speak and write directly to them.

Let me give you an example.

My avatar is a man named James between the ages of twenty-five and fifty-five. He's well educated, makes good money, has a wife, two to three kids, and he hates his job. He's overworked, unappreciated, and can see that things aren't going according to the plan he laid out when he signed on the corporate "dotted" line. James knows that the corporate ladder doesn't exist, and he'll never be able to retire if things keep going as they are. James sees the writing on the wall and knows that things won't "get better" just because his boss tells him they will. He wants to start his own business but doesn't have the time to figure out how. James knows he has talent and a certain level of expertise, but he doesn't quite know how to turn that into a business that will support his family. He has disposable income, subscribes to technology and startup-related magazines, and isn't afraid to spend some extra money to have nicer things.

Do you see how this level of specificity could help you target the people who would get the most value from your business? Whenever I write a blog post to James, although he's fictional, *real* people are impacted.

The more I know about "James," the better I can create products and services that would meet his needs and help solve his problems. Since I know James doesn't want to climb the (fictional) corporate ladder, I don't have to try to help him do it. Because I know he's busy, I can create content that saves him time and helps him get more done with the time he does have.

As you define your avatar, you're creating an "ideal" customer. This ideal is the center from which your audience will radiate.

For example, if your ideal client avatar is 35 years old, someone age 36 would be one standard deviation from the ideal. If they were 37, they'd be two standard deviations, etc.

If your avatar is a 32-year-old female *with* kids, a 35-year-old male *without* kids would be five deviations (three for the age difference, one for being male, and another for not having kids).

If you were to create a graph of your audience, it would look somewhat like this. Your avatar is in the middle with standard deviations of your avatar to the left and right; all of them together make up your audience

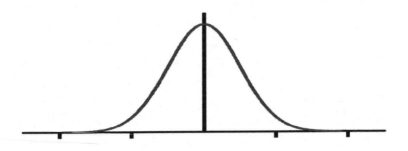

Figure 1 The Avatar Bell Curve

The closer someone is to the center line, the more likely they are to connect with you, your message, and what you're offering. They're also more likely to buy.

In my business, "James" is that middle vertical line. The more like him you are, the closer to the center line you'd be on this graph. A sixty-five-year-old retired female would be far to the right as an eighteen-year-old male might be off to the left.

I'm not suggesting you assign a point value to every member of your audience and plot where they fall on the Avatar Bell Curve. However, if you keep this visual in mind, you'll feel better when someone who isn't ideal (i.e., far left or right of center), declines to purchase your services.

I've personally found this Avatar Bell Curve to be very freeing. Since I know who is inside the curve, I know who to focus on. Anyone outside of the curve is a person who can't hurt my feelings when they cancel subscriptions, unsubscribe, or never hire me. Since they're not someone I'm targeting in the first place, no problem, nothing lost and no hard feelings.

How to Define Your Ideal Client Avatar

Below you'll find a list of questions I ask about my avatar every time I start to create a new product. I also have my coaching clients ask these questions when they're struggling to get traction with their audience.

I recommend you answer the following questions in as much detail as possible. The better you answer these questions, the better you can answer the more detailed "bonus" questions and the more targeted you can be with your marketing and content creation efforts. After you've answered these questions, you'll have a good idea of who your ideal client is and how you can target them.

Ask yourself:

- What does my avatar think about?

- How did they get where they are in life?

- How did they get where they are in their business/career?

- What *type* of work (manual, mental, advising, teaching) does my avatar do for employment?

- Where do they work?

- What does my avatar fear?

- What do they worry about?

- What are my avatar's goals?

- Who are their competitors?

- How did they learn their skills or their trade?

- What does my avatar spend their money on?

- What tools or types of devices, do they use?

- What social networks are they on?

- Where do they live?

- What kind of car do they drive? And why?

- Where do they work?

- Do they commute?

- If they commute, how far?

- What kind of clothes do they wear?

- What are my avatar's hobbies?

- What's their annual salary or household income?

Once you've answered the questions above, yes, all of them, in as much detail as possible, ask yourself the following "bonus" questions to help you really understand your avatar's habits:

- Who buys from my avatar? Who are my clients' clients?

- What does my avatar need?

- What does my avatar *think* they need?

- What problems is my avatar facing?

- What products and services is my avatar currently buying?

You don't have to try and reach everyone with your message, and that's ok. By narrowing your focus, you'll spend less time attracting the wrong kind of people, spend less money on marketing that isn't relevant to your avatar, and you'll be able to deliver an effective punch that will move your business forward.

If you want more training on how to identify your ideal client avatar, you can download a free PDF worksheet by going to www.ellorywells.com/lp/ideal.

31: SIGNING YOUR FIRST CLIENT

The critical ingredient is getting off your butt and doing something. It's as simple as that. A lot of people have ideas, but there are few who decide to do something about them now. Not tomorrow. Not next week. But today. The true entrepreneur is a doer, not a dreamer.
- Nolan Bushnell

After getting tossed head first into the world of entrepreneurship, I was forced to sink or swim. Unlike some famous entrepreneurs, I never thought I would start (much less own) my own business. Besides the detective agency I mentioned before, I've never given business ownership much thought. In the early days of working for IBM and Dell, I thought I'd retire at each of those companies. At Dell specifically, I was doing what I loved and making great money while doing it.

As I continued to read and study personal development books, I continued to grow as a person. And, as I grew, I blogged about it. Almost every post I wrote was a mix of personal stories and information distilled from leadership and entrepreneurship experts.

In the beginning, my posts came inconsistently. There was no set schedule or agenda. It wasn't until I'd been blogging for over a year that I began to develop a content strategy or started using a blog template. I wrote what I knew and shared about my journey of personal growth and development.

Time and time again I meet entrepreneurs who had a start similar to mine. By sharing their knowledge with their audience, they showed their expertise. In showing their trials and mistakes, they showed they were human and willing to put in the effort to become experts in their fields.

Sharing your missteps and mistakes through blogging, podcasting, creating videos, etc., doesn't harm your brand, it enhances it. The percentage of people who are willing to pull back the curtain, be vulnerable and connect with others in a real and honest way are the ones who will succeed.

Your prospective customers and clients may not relate to your successes, but they will be able to connect with your struggle. I remember reading Mark Cuban's autobiographical story which he published on his site, BlogMaverick.com.[40] He told the story of working for a small computer company, getting fired, and living on a friend's couch while trying to build a tech company. We may not be able to relate to Cuban's billions of dollars, but we can relate to his hustle.

Share your work, drive, and passion, and people will connect with you. Share your struggle in a way that helps other people through theirs, and they'll want to hire you. Share it often enough and with enough people and you have a business.

---

[40] http://www.blogmaverick.com/2009/05/13/success-motivation/

Tanaya

My first coaching client wasn't someone I recruited. She wasn't someone who had seen my coaching page full of testimonials and results and then decided to hire me. She was a single mom who had seen my posts on Facebook, followed the link, and read my blog. Over the course of a year and a half, I shared lessons and stories with her without even knowing it.

On the evening of April 15, 2013, my reader decided to send me the message below:

Tanaya ▆▆▆▆▆   Apr 15, 2013 9:59pm
Mr. Wells, I think you might be my coach, career mentor... I need one- BAD!!
I'm wanting to launch my business but need major, super help. I know what to do, I have what it takes, I just need a structure and a coach.

I'll admit that procrastination is a weakness of mine BUT only because I'm so busy with everything that I'm just trying to stay above water most times...
My passion, however is to "Do my own thing!!" Hopefully, I can do things my way and provide a better, more consistent life for me and those close to me.

Our connection (yours and mine):
1. Ashley and I worked together at KinderCare just before you two were married. Beautiful woman! I think I may have met you at her bridal shower (I think).
2. I simply adore empoweringthe80percent!! Your ideas are so inspiring.

Help Ellory!!
If you can accept my idea and consult with me personally please tell me what the next step is...

Sincerely and thanks,
Tanaya

I couldn't believe what I was reading! A coach? A consultant? Neither of these things had ever crossed my mind when I started writing in 2012. But, there I was with a Facebook message asking for more of my time.

By the time Tanaya reached out to me, I had published over sixty articles and written tens of thousands of words on my blog. Over the course of fourteen months, I'd written enough content for someone to know, like and trust me and want to hire me. And that's what blogs are ideal for (among other things). Blogs are an excellent way to show people who you are, what you're about, and what you stand for.

In full disclosure, I had met Tanaya once before. She had worked with my wife Ashley years ago, and she and I may have met in passing after a wedding shower. That brief meeting may have had an impact on her decision to reach out to me, but maybe not. I'll share more examples with you later about other professionals getting their first client, and hint: there was almost no "cold-calling" or random chance involved.

After I got over the shock of Tanaya's message, I scrambled to figure out what to do next. I researched coaching programs, fees, how to structure the coaching experience and all sorts of things to help me help her.

What I learned after the fact was that none of those things were necessary. What was important was that I gave everything I could to her and poured as much value into her life as possible. As entrepreneurs or wannabe entrepreneurs, we can get so focused on *how* to do things that we forget *why* we're doing them.

Instead of debating about how to meet and how much to charge, focus on why the client came to you in the first place, and go all in on helping them get what they need. Instead of thinking about how little of yourself you have to give, consider providing the best possible experience for your client. And don't make the mistake I did of trying to be "aloof" or distant in an attempt to seem busier or more important than you are. The manufactured illusion of exclusivity will do more harm than good. You can't satisfy your second client until you've delivered for the first, and there's no better advertisement or endorsement for your business than an entirely satisfied customer!

Each of these lessons applies to you and whatever you're doing as well. If you want to build websites, create the best sites you possibly can. If you wish to write music, make each song as if it were going to be played at Carnegie Hall. If you want to sell healthy recipes, find the best possible ingredients and create a formula that would make Gordon Ramsey jealous.

Instead of focusing on what is in your contract, focus on going above and beyond and how you can create a "wow" experience. No person and no business has ever achieved greatness by doing strictly what they were contractually obligated to do. The details will likely work out in the end, and, even if you end up putting in more work than you get paid for, you'll have something you're proud of to show to your next client.

Your customer will care less about the final result and how much they paid, and more about how you made them feel through the process. And, if the client has to cancel or end their contract with you, let them. Fighting with them or arguing won't leave them with positive feelings about you. It's better to lose a little cash than have someone out in the world telling all of their friends (and the world via social media) about how you screwed them or ruined a relationship over $200.

When you're starting your business, your reputation is everything. Sometimes positive brand equity is better than financial capital in the bank.

Six months after we worked together, Tanaya left her job and started a successful business. She put her training to work and was able to build a company for which she had a passion and drive. And, as a bonus, she got to make a significant impact on the lives of her clients and their families.

First Client Case Studies

I didn't want you to take my word for it, so I asked some friends and fellow entrepreneurs if I could share their stories.

What you'll find on the next several pages are case studies of Cynthia, Dale, Tamara and John, and how they signed their first clients. Cynthia teaches social media marketing and Pinterest strategy; Dale hosts workshops that help men explore their masculinity and find their identity; Tamara owns a video production and movie company; John is a police officer turned business coach.

Instead of finding case studies to reinforce my argument that everyone should blog, I found entrepreneurs I admired and asked them how they found their first client. These four case studies will show you how these entrepreneurs got their businesses off the ground. In each example, I've asked them to share about their business, how they found and signed their first clients, and the process they took to get their prospect to know, like and trust them.

After reading how some of my friends started their businesses, my hope is that you'll be ready to kick things into gear and have your prospects sign on the dotted line.

Case Study: Cynthia Sanchez

At the beginning stages of my first podcast, The Empowered Podcast, I came across Cynthia Sanchez. She is a registered nurse turned Pinterest expert. She started a blog and a podcast to share her passion for pinning. Her slogan, "Don't just pin it, do it!" resonated so much with her audience that she was able to turn her knowledge into a business. Even though she wasn't technical and, like me, had never heard of or used WordPress before, she dove in and figured it out.

On the twentieth episode of my show, [41] I had the opportunity to share Cynthia's story with my listeners. Specifically, I wanted to know how she'd built her business and got her first client. Had she cold called? Was there a plan she had put into place that led prospects through a sales funnel? I had to find out.

One day, while getting her hair done, Cynthia showed her stylist a picture she'd found on Pinterest. The image showed an

---

[41] Listen to my interview with Cynthia at http://www.empoweredpodcast.com/20

example of how Cynthia wanted to have her hair styled. Instead of bringing in the latest issue of a fashion magazine, Cynthia used social media.

After getting her hair styled, Cynthia asked if she could leave her business card behind at the salon. A short time later, she received a phone call. An owner of a new business in town had seen Cynthia's card and called her to see if she'd be interested in helping them with their social media.

The owner saw the card, asked the stylist about Cynthia and her blog, and then decided to pick up the phone. Only after seeing who Cynthia was and reading her website did they make the decision to hire her. That's the power of blogging and giving information, tools, and resources away for free.

Case Study: Dale Thomas Vaughn

I know of only two people who have made it their life's work to help other men feel comfortable in their masculinity, and I'm fortunate to call them both "friend." One of those men is Dale Thomas Vaughn, the founder of The Empower Mentorship Institute.

Dale has focused on his avatar from the beginning. His desire? To help men, ages 25-60, feel comfortable being men who don't fit the over-the-top male stereotype so prevalent in today's culture. Dale's goal is to coach and mentor his clients on their way from "lost and isolated to connected and found." Everything Dale does, from his blog to his TEDx talks, to his adventure workshops, is focused on serving his avatar.

I got to know Dale through my wife, Ashley. They'd attended the same high school, and when Facebook gained popularity, they reconnected like so many of us do. When Ashley saw Dale's message on social media, and when Dale's TEDx talk [42] was released, she knew he was someone I should connect with. I was fortunate to interview Dale on my podcast, [43] and we've since become friends.

Dale's success and the growth of The Empower Mentorship Institute are great examples of how people are drawn to us when we have a strong message, we know who we're trying to reach, and we have a solution to a specific problem.

Q&A with Dale Thomas Vaughn

You have a very specific avatar. How do you define your ideal client?

My avatar is male, between ages 25 and 60. He is a well-rounded, outgoing introvert and a dormant or bored high achiever, who is equal parts philosopher and adventurer. He is hungry for rites of passage and is searching for meaning in his life. He's looking to find or restore balance and purpose to his life, and he's tired of feeling isolated by workaholism or the tough guy cliché.

Can you share the story of how you got your first client?

I hosted a preview call and invited my friends. I didn't think anyone would show up, but two guys did. Then I didn't think anyone would buy my offer, but both guys did.

-----

[42] How Great Men Think Alike, Dale Thomas Vaughn, TEDxSMU - https://www.youtube.com/watch?v=gZzUgRnc3ns

[43] Listen to my interview with Dale at https://www.ellorywells.com/ep87-power-of-purpose-dale-thomas-vaughn/

Who were these guys? How did they find you?

Both of those first clients were friends to whom I'd given away my content for free for years on my Men's Hikes. One of them found me through a girl he barely knew. She told him, "I think you might like this hike for other guys like you." He came out on New Year's Day to the hike, and we've been friends and now peer mentors since (that was four years ago).

Knowing what you know today, would you have done anything different then?

Yes, I would have told more people about the preview call.

Do you use a blog to help market your skills, expertise or business? If so, how effective of a tool is blogging?

I used a blog for a while, but it never yielded much, so I stopped. I now mainly do video, live video streaming, or speaking on stage. I believe any marketing, done well, will work, but it has to fit you and your brand.

If you don't like writing, don't blog. If you don't like being on camera, don't do video. If you don't like writing pithy one liners, don't do Twitter. Do what fits you and do it fully. I do speaking and live video situations well, so I've revamped, and now my entire marketing strategy is around those two avenues.

What advice or encouragement would you offer to help an aspiring entrepreneur?

There is a personal journey you need to know is coming. Business success is as much about personal awareness and goals as it is about professional skill.

Get as many mentors and accountability networks in place as you can. If you are ready to go out on your own, try to prepare yourself to live a different style of life. Yes, you'll have your freedom, but you'll also have complete responsibility for yourself, your actions and your results.

You can't do it alone, so just admit it up front and ask everyone you know for help.

To find more information about Dale Thomas Vaughn, his workshops for men, and The Empower Mentorship Institute, please visit www.dalethomasvaughn.com.

Case Study: Tamara Thompson

In 2011, Tamara Thompson started her video company Serious Take Productions while she still had another job. For the first year, in her words, she was a "one-woman show." Like many entrepreneurs who start businesses on the side, Tamara grew her business through referrals, one happy customer at a time.

Serious Take Productions specializes in video production involving creative storytelling. From storyboarding a concept, preproduction, production with creative cinematography, to post-production and editing.

I had the chance to meet Tamara at the Thrive conference in Las Vegas in 2015 where she and her team were shooting the behind the scenes and documentary footage for the event. They use creative tools and emerging technology like video drones to create branding trailers for businesses and entrepreneurs, and beautiful aerial view shots for businesses like real estate agencies, country clubs, golf courses, and wineries.

Tamara knows that any business who isn't looking to implement video into their marketing plans is not her company's target market. Instead of spending the time trying to convince prospective clients of the importance of video, they target people and businesses who already see its value.

Serious Take Productions may have started out as a side project for Tamara, but now she travels around the world and charges hundreds of dollars for a day's work.

Q&A with Tamara Thompson

Who is the ideal client for your company?

Our target avatar is someone who has already established their brand, who they are for their business, and are looking to take the next step with video marketing. We look for clients who want to share stories and are passionate about what they do.

Who was your first client? How did you position yourself so they'd feel confident hiring you?

Our first client was [a] 100% all natural cosmetics brand. They were very established with their brand and had been in business for over twenty years. However, they'd never gone for video marketing until I shared my passion for creative storytelling as a way of marketing.

As I mentioned before, much of my freelance video work came through referrals and word of mouth advertising. I was referred to my first large corporate client through a photographer who shot still images for another video client [whom] I worked with before.

After meeting with them, filming multiple makeup tutorials and shooting behind the scenes footage, they decided to bring me on board regularly. We continue to work with them to this day and have now been working together for over three years.

Do you use a blog to help market your skills, expertise or business? If so, how effective of a tool is blogging?

I used a blog during the beginning stages of my business and started gaining traction after a couple of years. Then, when I rebranded and changed the direction I was going with the company, I stopped.

Now we typically only blog for specific projects, but I do believe that blogging is the way to start gaining more of a reach with clients who are searching the internet for what you have to offer. Blogging is perfect for social media shares and exposure online. Though blogging isn't for me, it is valuable for many businesses, and definitely for entrepreneurs.

What advice or encouragement would you offer to help an aspiring entrepreneur?

All I can say is to take action. Do not be afraid to take that first step. If you don't try, you will never know what would have happened. I'm not scared to ask. I am not afraid of rejection or fear. I have made mistakes, and I learned from them to make myself better for my clients.

You also have to be readily available to showcase your strengths and what you have to offer. I worked as a video production manager for two years, before I started Serious Take. If you don't take action, work hard and connect with the right people, the process can be slow. Surround yourself with other entrepreneurs that will help lift you up as well as help lead you on your path.

To find more information about Tamara Thompson and how she uses Serious Take Productions to focus on creative storytelling, please go to www.serioustakeproductions.com

Case Study: "Catalyst" John McKee

If you walked up to me and asked, "Do you know John McKee?" I'd probably tell you "no." But ask me if I'm friends with Catalyst John, I'd have the pleasure of saying, "heck ya!"

"Catalyst" John McKee is a business and purpose coach, but he didn't start out as one. Before leaving to pursue his passion for helping people get results and live with purpose, John was a police officer.

But, even as a law enforcement officer, Catalyst John had a talent for training and teaching. He taught classes at church, trained crowd management and riot control, and soon became a sought-after instructor for [his] entire department.

As John puts it, "Even though I strapped on body armor every day and wore a gun on my hip, I had the heart of an entrepreneur. I loved training, but I was not sold out to life as a cop."

But it's ok that he had the heart of an entrepreneur stuck in the body of a police officer because, unlike me, John was born into entrepreneurship. His family owned several restaurants in John's hometown, and he'd grown up around the family business. Even while he was training officers and patrolling the streets of Florida as a policeman, John owned a screen printing company where he hand-printed custom t-shirts for local businesses.

After much prayer and many long talks with his wife, John decided to submit his two weeks notice to the force and register for one of Dan Miller's coaching classes. It was then that John decided to combine his talents as a teacher and his passion for helping other entrepreneurs, and turn them into a successful coaching business.

Without expecting to launch his company yet, John gave some advice to an aspiring entrepreneur named RJ. John had no product to sell and no services to offer, but he wanted to help. Not long afterward, John received a Facebook message from RJ, who now wanted to hire a coach to help him focus on building his business. After that, John focused on getting another client, then another, then another. It didn't take long for John to build a network and recruit clients around the world.

My friend Catalyst John is an excellent example of how we can achieve almost anything we set our mind too, and it's never too late to make a change so we can make a difference.

Q&A with "Catalyst" John

You've got a great story about how you got your first client. Can you share?

Absolutely! My first client, RJ, approached me. I was still trying to figure out my business and what it would look like, and inadvertently, my [first] client helped me understand my business model.

RJ's "day job" was in Computer Aided Design but he wanted to launch a business as a health coach. He'd had Chron's disease and beat it, and he was energized and eager to help other people suffering from the disease. He was a single guy with a career, but he wanted to live a life that wasn't controlled by his health condition.

My first contact with RJ had come a few weeks before he mentioned hiring me. I'd been invited to attend an event created by Seth Godin called an Icarus Session. Everyone attending was given the opportunity to stand up in front of the crowd and proclaim, "Here, I made this!"

RJ shared his story and vision for what he wanted to achieve with his business. After everyone had their chance to make their proclamation, and the meeting came to a close, I caught up with RJ in the hotel lobby.

Though I only knew a little bit about his plans, I said "Here are the things you must know, but no one will ever tell you about running a business."

I landed my first client because I knew I could tell him some things that would help him create more success when he launched his business. I honestly just wanted to help him win, and he saw that. A couple of weeks later, he reached out to me and said he wanted to hire me to help him grow his business.

The irony is, I wasn't a coach when I met RJ. I was a guy in transition to my purpose. The amazing thing I learned is that you don't have to be as far as you think to get started or before you reach out and offer to help.

I didn't have a business when my first client hired me. I didn't know the name of my company, I didn't have a website, and didn't even have a business card. All I had was the desire to solve a particular problem for someone in need, and it worked.

What do you think it was that made RJ feel like he could know/like/trust you?

He liked me because I was just being me. I built trust because when I gave him advice, it was great advice. I talked about what I knew, and it wasn't me trying to come up with advice. I just told him what I'd learned from my experiences in business and studying business.

About how much did you charge for your coaching service back then?

I charged $75 a session and we met at Starbucks. He got a full hour of coaching and a cup of coffee!

Do you use a blog to help market your skills, expertise or business? If so, how effective of a tool is blogging?

No, not really. I have a blog, but I don't write consistently. Most of my clients come through networking and referrals.

What advice or encouragement would you offer to help an aspiring entrepreneur?

Be authentic. Do something that burns inside of you. Help one person at a time and soon you can have a line of people wanting your help!

We screw up because we forget to help the person. At the beginning and end of every day, it is about helping our clients achieve a specific result.

To find more information about Catalyst John and to check out his coaching services, please go to www.catalystjohn.com.

***

As you can see from these case studies, blogging isn't the only way to build your business, even if that business is an online one. However, one strategy can be found in each of these case studies - giving value for free. Each of these business owners has followed the freemium model of building a business. The tactics may differ, one entrepreneur uses videos, one webinars, another provides free advice and relies on referrals, but they each create content that tells a story and converts visitors to clients.

Whether it's a free training or webinar, a sample of your work, a free consult or an adjustment like the chiropractor from before, the freemium model works.

Action Steps

Sharing your story and the adventure it contains is critical to the growth and success of your business. People will want to work with you, buy from you, watch and listen to you because of how you make them feel.

To sign your first client, you must convince them that you have what they need, and you can deliver what you promise. If you've deployed the strategy outlined in the Roadmap, you're now ready to start signing clients.

Here are the three things I've had success doing, and what I coach my clients to do when they're ready to start making money.

Step 1: Create a Prototype

As Henry Ford said, "You can't build a reputation on what you're going to do." You have to create before you can collect. Put out great content, paint wonderful paintings, make delicious donuts, shoot amazing videos, and give many of them away for free. And keep getting better. Always keep improving on your skills and revamping and revising your original work.

Create a prototype for what you'd like your client to buy. That prototype could come in the form of a blog post outlining how you've achieved a certain result. It could be a web design template you'd like to use for clients. Or, it could be the physical item you'd like to sell on a larger scale.

The more clear and defined your prototype, the more likely you are to sell it. Alternatively, the more the prospect has to use their imagination the less likely or excited they'll be about parting with their hard-earned dollars

Step 2: Share Your Work

While watching the 2013 movie *Jobs,* starring Ashton Kutcher, I noticed something interesting in the way Steve behaved while building their business. Instead of toiling away, hidden in their Palo Alto garage, Steve Jobs called dozens, no, hundreds of potential investors, business owners, and local computer stores.

Jobs told them he and Wozniak were building something that would change the world. He asked them for orders, asked them to invest, and he asked them for the opportunity to share Apple's product with them.

Steve Jobs changed the world, and he did it by creating something amazing and sharing that creation. Had Jobs never left his garage, the world might have never known the iPhone, iPad, or other amazing devices that have changed our lives.

To build your business, you have to be your own fan club, your own salesman, and your own marketing department. If you believe your product or service is the water that thirsty people need, you shouldn't have a problem sharing it with the world.

Step 3: Ask for the Sale

A few months ago, my neighborhood's Home Owners Association held a small business fair in the parking lot of one of our rec centers. Since I work with businesses and entrepreneurs, I wanted to go and see who I could meet.

But, I'd slept late, and it was raining, and by the time I left the house I wondered how many businesses would still be manning their booths. When I pulled into the parking lot, I saw a small push cart giving away coffee, a tent with handmade donuts, and a table covered with an odd-looking assortment of jewelry. Most of the businesses had folded up their tables, packed it in and left.

Since I hadn't yet had my fix of caffeine, I made a beeline for the coffee cart and asked if they could make me a Caramel Machiatto, my favorite. After picking up my drink with two extra shots of espresso, I set out to explore the other booths.

Just a moment later, a woman asked me if I'd like to try one of her donuts. Together, with her were her mom and her cousin, she was planning to open a new donut shop at the beginning of the summer, and they were here to promote their featured product, donuts.

I enjoyed the donut and coffee, and when the donut shop opened on June first, I was right there to support them.

Whether you ask people to attend your event, to sample your product, listen to a podcast or read a blog post, you must ask people to support you. Had the lady never asked me to try her donuts, I might never have stopped into her store.

Consumers have more options today than ever before. New businesses are popping up all over the place, and competition is fierce. If you want to make a sale, you'll have to ask for it, and you might have to ask more than once.

Give freely. Don't be afraid to put in the work up front so you can bring people in the door later. Share your work and invite people to try it for themselves.

32: THE BEGINNING

Be so good they can't ignore you.
- Cliff Ravenscraft

The world needs more entrepreneurs. We need risk-takers, pioneers, and people who are willing to break from the status quo and do something amazing.

Your journey begins here, and the road only gets more difficult. People will tease you and tell you "it can't be done." Your friends will change, and some of them might even attempt to talk you out of trying to achieve your dream. Don't let the limitations of others keep you from going after what you want. Guard your mind against negativity and surround yourself with people who will encourage you, support you, challenge you and help you become the best version of yourself.

Taking a Punch

My wife and I enjoy watching the fighters of the Ultimate Fighting Championship on television. Those athletes are experts at what they do and are masters of their craft many of them holding advanced belts in multiple styles of figthing.

But one thing every fighter must face when they step into the ring is the fact that they're going to have to take a punch. No matter how good or well prepared they are, they know they're going to get hit.

As you start, build and grow your business, you too will get hit. Maybe your punch will come from a friend or a loved one who is unwilling to support you. Maybe it will come from a bank that denies a loan at a critical juncture. And maybe your hardest hit will come from the self-doubt that accompanies doing anything difficult and worth doing.

You will get hit. You will have to take a punch.

But you're strong. You're prepared. And you have a team around you willing to step in and help you get back up and move forward.

Like the fighter who accepts the reality of taking a punch, you too must accept the fact that things will go wrong, and you'll have some days when nothing seems to go according to plan. Achieving your dream and building your business will take time and more effort than you think.

But you've got this.

I believe in you.

Now get to work.

THE BEGINNING

PART V - APPENDICES

APPENDIX A: RECOMMENDED READING LIST

If you don't have time to read, you don't have the time (or the tools) to write. Simple as that.
- Stephen King

The man who does not read has no advantage over the man who cannot read.
- Mark Twain

Please proceed with caution. If you read these books, you'll begin to see the world in a whole new way. You'll see new possibilities and learn new things. You will start to see that a better world is out there if you're willing to create it. Personal development books don't come with a warning label, but they should. By reading these books, you agree to take full responsibility for what happens next. You have been warned.

If you'd prefer this list with clickable links, you can find it at www.theexitstrategybook.com/appendix-a/.

In alphabetical order:

Drive by Daniel Pink

EntreLeadership by Dave Ramsey

Flight of the Buffalo by James A. Belasco and Ralph C. Stayer

✓ *How to Win Friends and Influence People* by Dale Carnegie

Leadership and Self-Deception by The Arbinger Institute

✓ *Outliers* by Malcolm Gladwell

✓ *Platform* by Michael Hyatt

Quitter by Jon Acuff

✓ *Start* by Jon Acuff

Stop Chasing Influencers by Kimanzi Constable and Jared Easley

✓ *The 21 Irrefutable Laws of Leadership* by John C. Maxwell

✓ *The 7 Habits of Highly Effective People* by Stephen Covey

✓ *The E-Myth Revisited* by Michael Gerber

The Icarus Deception by Seth Godin

The Invisible Selling Machine by Ryan Deiss

✓ *The Millionaire Fastlane* by MJ DeMarco

✓ *The Millionaire Messenger* by Brendon Burchard

The Power of Positive Living by Norman Vincent Peale

✓ *The Slight Edge* by Jeff Olson

✓ *The War of Art* by Steven Pressfield

Think and Grow Rich by Napoleon Hill

To Sell is Human by Daniel Pink

Writing Riches by Ray Edwards

APPENDIX B: RECOMMENDED TOOLS & RESOURCES

What follows is a list of the tools and resources I either use currently, have used in the past or, on the rare occasion, have not used but trust the tool.

You can also find each of the tools listed below (with hyperlinks) at www.theexitstrategybook.com/appendix-b.

Social Media Tools

1. **Buffer** - www.bufferapp.com

2. **HootSuite** - www.hootsuite.com

3. **Pablo by Buffer** - www.bufferapp.com/pablo

4. **Bulk Buffer** (scheduling in bulk) - www.bulkbuffer.com

Platform Building Tools

1. **WordPress** - www.wordpress.com (Free)

2. **WordPress** - www.wordpress.org (For installing on your own domain, recommended)

3. **Bluehost** - www.theexitstrategybook.com/hosting (Website hosting)

4. **StudioPress** - www.theexitstrategybook.com/themes (Premium WordPress themes & Professional design)

5. **OptimizePress** - www.theexitstrategybook.com/landingpages (Landing, sales, thank you and webinar pages, Membership and restricted access tools)

Email Marketing Tools

1. **ActiveCampaign** - www.theexitstrategybook.com/activecampaign

2. **MailChimp** - www.theexitstrategybook.com/mailchimp

3. **Email Spam Scoring Tool** - www.mail-tester.com

E-Commerce Tools

1. **Easy Digital Downloads** - www.easydigitaldownloads.com

2. **WooCommerce** - www.woothemes.com/woocommerce

3. **PayPal** - www.paypal.com

4. **Stripe** - www.stripe.com

Writing Tools

1. **Hemingway App -**
   www.theexitstrategybook.com/hemingway

2. **Grammarly** - www.theexitstrategybook.com/grammarly

Receive exclusive updates and become an official Strategist!

Get the most out of *Exit Strategy* and share your success story with the community by visiting

www.theexitstrategybook.com/join

Ellory Wells is a writer and a coach. From an early age, Ellory recognized his ability to connect people and build a successful team, even from a group of castaways and the third string players of the "C-Team." He still remembers the nauseating feeling of logging into his work computer while miserable in Corporate America, and his goal is to help people avoid that same feeling. Ellory and his wife, Ashley, live in the Austin, Texas suburb of Round Rock where Ashley is a cardiac sonographer. You can connect with Ellory on his website at www.ellorywells.com.

Made in the USA
San Bernardino, CA
17 November 2016